Diabolical in Disguise

A True Story of Resilience

Jessica Solsona

Copyright © 2023 Jessica Solsona
All rights reserved
First Edition

PAGE PUBLISHING
Conneaut Lake, PA

First originally published by Page Publishing 2023

DISCLAIMER:
This book is based on true events in my life.
However, it has been fictionalized, and all persons
appearing in this work are fictional.
Any resemblance to real people, living or dead, is entirely
coincidental. Events in this book could be trigger-sensitive.

ISBN 979-8-88960-635-2 (pbk)
ISBN 979-8-88960-686-4 (hc)
ISBN 979-8-88960-648-2 (digital)

Printed in the United States of America

To my children, Jake, Emilce, Isabelle, and Evelynn: You are my purpose in life. I am so amazed at how down-to-earth and strong you kids are. You make me proud because you guys know who you are, you know when people are doing right and wrong, and you each have so much to offer this world. Continue to speak out for yourselves and others.

To Guillermo: Ever since I began my journey of speaking out and telling my truth, you have always been an amazing supporter.

To my sweet daughter Emilce: You left too soon. I am thankful to have had a chance to have you in my life. You taught me so much—to see the beauty in everything, to have patience, to be kind, and to have an entrepreneurial mind. Not only were you my daughter, but you were also my best friend. You will be in my heart and soul forever. I love you!

Emilce Borbon was born on January 26, 1999. Her life was cut short after a battle with leukemia on June 28, 2014.

Contents

Preface vii
Introduction ix
Chapter 1: Diabolical in Disguise 1
Chapter 2: My Guardian Candy Canes 6
Chapter 3: Sunny California 11
Chapter 4: Where Will Home Be Tomorrow? 16
Chapter 5: Just over the Bridge 27
Chapter 6: My First Boyfriend 41
Chapter 7: Trip to Juvenile Hall 47
Chapter 8: Escort Life of a Teen 53
Chapter 9: Married at Fifteen 60
Chapter 10: A Child Who Changed My Life 66
Chapter 11: Having a Child Never Changed His Ways 70
Chapter 12: Brainwashing 79
Chapter 13: What Is the Right Choice? 85
Chapter 14: Life in Costa Rica 90
Chapter 15: Family Sunday Dinner 95
Chapter 16: Waking Up in a Barn 97
Chapter 17: My Sweet Baby Girl Was Sick 101
Chapter 18: Freedom at Twenty-One 105
Chapter 19: The Job That Changed It All 114
Chapter 20: A Wonderful Man 122
Chapter 21: Working on Me 125
Chapter 22: Grieving 130
Chapter 23: What I Have Learned through It All 135

Preface

This is the story of how I survived being molested, abused, hated, and neglected and the fight to protect my children from a cycle of abuse that began during my childhood. It is a story of how I grieved my daughter who passed away from leukemia at fifteen years old. This is my story of how I stayed resilient and broke free from the cycle of abuse.

Introduction

You may be asking yourself, "Why does she have the urge to tell her story?" Many people have told me that I'm just victimizing myself by speaking out, that I am just looking for attention, that they are better than me because they don't relive their past over and over, that these types of things happen to all of us and they don't talk about it, or that I'm not special simply because I wrote this book and spoke out. Those people don't know what it's like to hide a previous or current secret life, never telling a soul in fear of being judged or doubted.

After twenty-one years, I escaped the vicious cycle of abuse that started during my childhood. I dealt with so many ups and downs with complex PTSD, depression, anxiety, panic attacks, extreme anguish, and not knowing who I was for the longest time. It took me so much education and determination to get better in order to live a "normal life" with healthy relationships. I am proud that I fought to better my life for my family. I am not afraid anymore and will continue speaking my truth. I want my voice heard loud and clear in order to help at least one person break their cycle of abuse. I want my story to inspire others so they can find their self-worth, fight for freedom, and work hard for the life they deserve!

Chapter 1

Diabolical in Disguise

I was born on February 22, 1979, in Twin Falls, Idaho. I have an older brother named Pete, who was born in 1978. I was born healthy, except for a cleft palate and hearing problems. I was about six months old when I had my first surgery to close my cleft palate because whenever I ate, the food went through the roof of my mouth and out my nose when I swallowed.

I was unable to hear clearly because the tubes in my ears were not connected correctly to my eardrums. When I was around a year old, I had my first surgery on my ears to insert tubes. From there on, my hearing got better, but I had lots of ear infections.

During the first few years of my life, my mother worked at a potato factory while my father cooked in a restaurant. My grandmother from my mother's side came to visit when I was around a year old, and as I have been told, there was no food in the house, so she stocked the refrigerator for us. She warned my mother and father that the conditions we were living in were not suitable for children.

Soon afterward, my mother left my father, enlisted in the Army, and took my brother Pete and me to live on the base she was stationed in Texas. We stayed on the base for about six months until the day my brother opened the front door while our mother was in the shower, and we went outside to play in a mud puddle near the freeway. Thankfully, we weren't kidnapped or hit by an oncoming car. A trucker brought us home before anything bad could happen. After that, we were no longer allowed to stay on base with her, so my grandmother picked us up and took us to live with her in California.

My brother and I loved our grandparents' house. Grandma prepared everything fresh, from bread to jelly. Her tomato soup was my all-time favorite. She made us breakfast, lunch, and dinner, with snacks in between. We played like kids without worry, so happy to be living in a safe and loving environment. Pete and I stayed with them until I was around five years old.

My mother met a man named Earl while she was enlisted in the Army. Once their terms in the service were over, they came to get me and Pete from our grandparents' house. Earl married our mother and became our stepfather. He had two children from a previous marriage, and they had one child together named Vanessa.

We were now a family of three girls and two boys. I never really had a close relationship with Earl's kids except my half sister, Vanessa. I loved spending time with her and felt I had to be a role model or a nurturing figure for her, which made me feel important. My biological brother, Pete, was distant at the time we moved into Earl's home. I also ended up having a few more surgeries on my ears in Oakland, California.

I was around six years old when we moved from California to Missouri to live in a house so huge they had a maid to do the cleaning. Whenever I walked around our home, there was always a slightly disturbing, cold, quiet vibe. The atmosphere outside was very dark, rainy, and gloomy all the time. I missed my grandparents' home back in California, where it was sunny and felt safe.

Our household was very strict and military-like. If we ever looked into our parents' eyes, they saw that as a symbol of defiance and a form of disrespect. After watching Earl backhand his son for looking directly into Earl's eyes and speaking, I realized it was as if that meant we had confidence, so they broke it by not allowing us to speak out with confidence or look into the eyes of authority. I learned my lesson quickly and was always too nervous to look them in the eyes when they spoke to me, so this rule was an easy one for me.

"Yes, sir" and "Yes, ma'am" were required, and it was a rule that we didn't ever want to forget. We had to be excused to use the restroom and to leave the table. We all washed our own dishes, cleaned the kitchen, and were then sent off to our rooms after dinner. Our rooms had to be spotless before we left them in the morning; I would hear Earl walking down the hall, going room to room.

As I sat there on my bed, waiting my turn, the anticipation was unbearable. I felt so afraid that my room might not be clean enough. When he got to my room and I saw him with my own eyes, my heart dropped. I could not breathe, and I felt like passing out. If it was clean enough, we were excused from playing outside. I guess living with military parents meant it was the way we were going to be raised. During this time, I ended up having another surgery on my ears and had new tubes put in. My hearing and ear infections were bad at times.

I was feeding my sister Vanessa, who was about ten months old at the time, when I heard Earl's feet stomping toward me from behind. He grabbed me by my hair and dragged me toward the master bedroom. I remember looking down at the ground, seeing how far away it was as he held me by my hair. I had a distinct feeling that this had happened before. It was foggy, but maybe I could not remember because I was so young or did not want to remember.

He threw me in the tile shower stall, and I found out why he was angry: someone had left a washcloth in the shower. The rule was that we put our washcloths in the washroom every time we got out of the shower. I don't know what happened to me after that, but the next thing I remember was waking up in bed next to my mother crying and petting my hair. I had a bad headache and felt dizzy when I stood up. I went to the bathroom, and when I looked in the mirror, I saw my face was bruised, and my hair was falling out from where he had grabbed hold of it.

I was so confused and afraid because I could only remember very little of what happened that day. My mother never comforted me like that again, the way she did that night. Her tears were the only real caring emotion she had ever shown me. I knew that Earl must have done something bad if I was unable to remember.

Things became very different, very quickly, after that. My mother had gone to college for massage therapy, and I found out later in life that my stepfather had gotten her into the escort industry around that time. She worked at a massage parlor, providing the type of service that comes with a happy ending. She was busy working night shifts, and he liked it like that.

I felt so alone because no one paid any mind to me, what I was feeling or what I was going through in my struggle to hear. At times, my hearing was good; other days, it was bad. I had to blow up four to six balloons a day after the surgeries on my ears so they would "pop" and not close. I had many painful ear infections from it, but popping my ears was necessary to hear as best I could each day.

One night, as I lay in my bed, I heard ice being dropped into a glass cup, a splash hitting the ice cubes, and then soda being opened and poured into the glass of ice. That noise it made when opened, the sizzle it made when poured, the ice-popping noise when soda hit ice cubes, and the noise as he stirred the drink with his two fingers and sucked them afterward is something I will never forget. I knew he was coming down the hallway because I could hear his footsteps approaching my room.

My body went numb, and butterflies flitted in my stomach. I felt like peeing on my bed the closer he got because I did not know why he was coming to my room, and I had a feeling it was not to say goodnight.

Earl came into my room and asked me if I had any panties on. I said, "Yes." He ordered me to take them off, and I did with fear. I had no idea what was going to happen when he carried me off to the living room. There were naked people on TV, rubbing all over each other and making strange noises. He laid me next to him as he put his fingers on my private parts.

I was afraid and felt sick. I knew if I said anything, he would hurt me. I felt so disgusting inside as I lay there until he was done, trying my hardest not to cry. When he was finished, he asked me if I liked it, but I didn't answer. I asked him if I could be excused and go back to bed. He finally let me go back to my room. I was in shock from what had happened and felt it was not real. I hoped it was all a bad dream. I did not want it to be true that my innocence had just been ripped from me, this five-year-old girl who was only beginning life. The reality is, that night, he changed my whole life forever. He did not hurt me by accident, nor did he resent what he had done. The reality of my world became darker than it had ever been from that point on.

Chapter 2

My Guardian Candy Canes

THE MOLESTATION HAPPENED EVERY NIGHT FROM THEN on. One of those nights, I went to bed and hid under the covers and said to myself, "I am not scared! I am not scared!" As I fell asleep, I had this dream that a king gnome came out of the closet with a lot of other gnomes following behind. The king had a cane with a crystal ball at the tip of it.

The king gnome asked me if I was scared, and I shook with fear and whispered, "No!" If he did not believe me, he beat me with his cane. After that, I kept having the same dream every night. I ended up having more confidence and not being scared. The king gnome never beat me again. I learned to hide my fears and shield my emotions. Becoming numb was the only way not to be frightened.

As time went on, I had a guardian who would sit at my window every night and protect me. He was my only friend, and I named him Candy Canes because he was very kind. I made him out of clay one time because my teacher asked me to show her what I had been talking to in class, and she wanted to know what it looked like. She looked at me differently like with concern, as I told her that it protected me from mean people.

I used to imagine that Candy Canes would shield me while bad things were happening to me, and then it didn't hurt so bad. As weird as it sounds, I knew my body was just a body, and I wanted my soul to be protected.

Candy Canes may have looked devilish, but he was a beastly protector who was there for me. It was those who were hiding behind their masks and evil intentions and doings who were the real diabolical in disguise. Growing up, I always wondered if all children who were neglected and afraid of being alone had protectors. Without him, I don't know how I would have made it through all the abuse.

I was always on edge about what I was going to be punished for next. No matter how perfectly I made my room or picked up after myself, there was always something I was in trouble for. The funny thing was, I never imagined getting myself out of that life. I just thought that was life, the way it would always be.

One day, when we were on our way to Burger King, I couldn't say the name right. I said, "Bugger King," because it was hard for me to pronounce it correctly, and my stepfather made me sit in the car while they all ate inside since I couldn't say it right. I was so hungry that day, and they all ate without me, acting like I didn't exist. I hated myself because my family did not accept me, and it seemed I couldn't do anything right.

I spent a lot of my childhood in silence, afraid to talk to anyone because I stuttered and couldn't speak correctly. I tried my hardest not to stutter when I talked, and I made sure all my things were picked up, but I was always getting in trouble for something.

One day, when Earl was beating my mom, he announced, "All of you kids need to stand in line and watch." I thought it was a typical day, but something was different. We did as we were told and lined up in the kitchen. I didn't want to look, and neither did they, but he made us. He said, "This is the way you treat a woman." He then told my brother, who was around seven years old at the time, "Get me some rope from the garage." My mother was huddled on the floor, crying and begging for Earl to stop. When Pete came back, Earl told him, "Sit down, watch, and learn."

We watched as he placed her in a chair, her hair a mess and her face red and swollen from being smashed into the floor countless times. Tears were rolling down her face, with snot coming out of her nose—she looked so tired and weak. My mother was very petite compared to my stepfather's muscular frame.

He ordered Pete to wrap the rope around our mother, and Earl made sure it was tight. We all stood there in silence, for if we were to make a sound, we knew he would become more violent. We were all helpless as he punched her in the face and screamed at her. The disgusting scene was not over until he was "finished," and only then were we dismissed.

Then he told our mother to take a shower, like nothing had happened, just an ordinary Sunday afternoon—I guess it was. To this day, my brother feels guilty for listening to Earl, feeling he could have said no or done something different to change the fact that he'd helped Earl tie up our mother, but there really wasn't anything he could have done except obey.

The sexual, physical, and emotional abuse I was experiencing at home made me quiet and withdrawn, not trusting a soul. I had to go to school like everyone else, but since my hearing issues had impaired my speech, I was in a special-education class at the time. I had six surgeries throughout the years to repair my eardrums, and my last surgery was when I was around eight years old.

I hated it when teachers would touch my back as they wandered about the room looking at everyone's schoolwork—you know, the soft rub to try to comfort you as they whisper in your ear, "Good job," or, "How are you feeling today?" I hated it because they didn't know me, what I was currently going through, or how I felt about anything.

That action made me feel as if they were trying to manipulate me, trying to gain my trust so I would tell them my feelings and have them judge me. I brushed off their touches when they walked away. Whether they touched my arm or my back, I felt a tingly sensation and couldn't wait for them to leave so I could wipe that feeling of disgust from my body. I made sure no one noticed so they wouldn't ask me why I did that and so they wouldn't think I was weird.

After my enduring years of sexual abuse from Earl, it all ended one night. Our nanny happened to be working late while my stepfather was performing his nightly ritual. She saw him molesting me and called the police. Years of torment ended with one phone call—a single call.

They asked my mother if she knew anything about this, and my mother denied it all! She said that she had no way of knowing this was going on. She knew and would get upset when he did it in front of her, not because he was hurting me but because she was sick with jealousy.

He would stick his tongue in my mouth, and all she would say to him was "Okay, that's enough, Earl." She said she hated me because I was stealing her husband, and he paid more attention to me than her. I was a little girl and wanted my mom to protect me, yet the only thing she gave me was hate.

I went to the hospital, and they asked me all these questions like, "Where did he touch you? How long did this happen? Was it every night? Were there other children who were molested or abused in the home or out of the home that you knew about?" They had dolls with all the private parts. I had to show them all the things he had done to me. I did not want to explain it to people I did not know, and I did not understand how to tell them. I was not allowed to express my feelings. It was hard to understand at that age if I was safe and allowed to tell.

My mom got away with leading them to believe she would have never put her kids into that kind of life, acting so innocent. I guess women are more believable when they are small, have a sweet voice and big puppy-dog eyes, dress sexy, and act like the victim. He went to jail, and we had to sell everything to move close to her mother in California. She did not tell the real story to her parents.

She told them he had touched Vanessa, putting his finger in her diaper once, so she left. She loved my sister and never allowed anything bad to happen to her because she was the blood of the man she loved, I guess. I was beaten by my mom, and I was told she hated me every day! I was told it was my fault he went to jail and I was a slut for trying to steal her husband. I never understood why she thought this way.

I was not allowed to talk to my grandma or grandpa about anything, and when they bought me a gift, it would be ripped up and thrown in the garbage by my mom. I ended up not showing that I liked anything, knowing that if I liked something and she knew it, it would be destroyed.

Things between my mother and me only got worse now that she hated me even more for Earl's absence. I had screwed up her perfect life. She was more than willing to sacrifice my innocence to keep living the expensive lifestyle, or I suppose maybe she loved the kind of control that felt addictive. She seemed so lost and afraid without Earl.

She looked dissociated and in shock. I knew she was crazy, and I also knew this was the start of her taking her craziness to a whole new level. I prepared for the worst.

I was thankful that I was not getting molested at night. The only bad thing was my mom was upset most of the time and would wake me up in the middle of the night to beat me and tell me how much I had ruined her life.

I always thought I was cursed by an evil spell or maybe God really hated me in a past life and was punishing me in this life. There was no ending to hell. I tried to sing a song or imagine something just to make time pass by while she beat and screamed at me so I would not feel the pain or hear her hurtful words that ripped my soul.

I then learned how to sleep with one eye open, so I was prepared for her beatings and hurtful words. School was the only place I could be at peace and take short naps if I was lucky. I was allowed to lay my head on my desk if I did all my classwork.

Chapter 3

Sunny California

AFTER WE MOVED TO CALIFORNIA, MY MOTHER continued to work as an escort, but this time from home during the day. At night, she made her appointments elsewhere. She had us kids stay in our rooms for hours at a time while her clients were there, and we dared not make a single noise.

I would hear her talking and laughing with strange men and listen to their footsteps walking about the house. After they left, she would let us out. If my mother was happy with the amount of money she made in a day, then she mostly left me alone.

When I was nine, I saw my mother in her room with the lights off and candles lit; she was mumbling a prayer. After I got to my room, she came in and said that there were three men who had told her to kill me and that she wished I were dead. She told me how much she hated me because I was responsible for her losing the man she loved. She pulled my hair, slammed me to the ground, and kept hitting my face on the floor. "You ruined my life! If it weren't for you, I'd still be with him!" she screamed.

She would not stop kicking me in the stomach, and I lay there until she was satisfied with the savage beating she had given me. I was asked to clean up and take a cold shower. I hated my life and wished she would have killed me at that point.

Special education was easy for me in fourth grade, and I finished my schoolwork quickly. All the girls in my class were friendly, but the boys were annoying and mean. My friends would always come to me if a boy hit them or was picking on them, and I would protect them. Once, the girls ran up to me and told me to protect them from this boy who was being mean to them. They called me "Supergirl!" Everyone was playing around, and I played along with them. They gave me a sense of importance and strength in my otherwise-powerless existence. When I was in school, it gave me a break from all the abuse in the home.

Then I would be on the bus on my way home and feel like peeing my pants, my heart racing, and my body becoming numb all over. I was so scared of being beaten that my body did not know how to react. I wished for my mom to be drinking her wine and eating her favorite food. I hoped that the house was clean enough for her. Most of all, I wished that she had made money that day.

She would get home from working at the spa, where she made all her appointments at night. I would hear her turn the key in the door, always in a certain way that told me whether she had a great day or was going to get me. She would look around the house and go through all the rooms. I could hear her high heels as they hit the wood floor going toward my room. *Here we go again*, I thought to myself. Was it the bathroom? Was it the kitchen? Maybe it was the living room that was not clean enough for her. Maybe something reminded her of what she could have had if she were still with my stepfather. She came to my room and dragged me by my hair out of bed. It felt as if my hair was ripping from my scalp. She would drag me to the place that was not clean enough for her.

Usually, it was the bathroom. She would slam my head into the toilet, keep hitting me, and scream, "See the toilet? It is not clean!" She would put my face in it and hit me over and over. When she ran out of breath, she would stop hitting me. I then had the feeling of my body thumping because of the painful hits. She spit on me after each beating as a way to finish it off.

She told me to take a cold shower. Then I had to stand in the corner the rest of the night. I often would look for figures and shapes on the wall. The stucco that was flattened had different shapes that looked like something: a horse, car, bike, person—I guess you get the point. There were so many different things on the wall that I never got bored with it. It also helped me not to go insane from standing there for so long. I felt it made the time fly by faster. I even learned how to sleep standing up.

Sometimes, I did not have to stand in the corner; she would leave me in the bathroom, and I would sleep in the bathtub or on the bathroom floor after her beatings. I was sometimes grateful that she let me stay there so I could at least sleep lying down. I was cold, and the tub was hard, but if I was lucky, there would be a towel in there to cover myself.

There was only one thing in my young life that I found pleasure in, and that was watching other children sing. It gave me a warm tingly feeling in my heart, a feeling of pure joy, and I felt like crying. They sang with love and passion. The happiness in their eyes made me wish I felt that way. I cried when watching the kids hug their parents, hearing the parents tell them how proud they were and how much they loved them. I began to hate everything. I hated the fact that those kids had the life I wanted, and I wished for loving parents. I would have changed shoes with anyone at that point in my life.

I never had a dad in my life who loved me and would protect me from bad. I started to listen to music from men, their raspy voices making me feel like I was safe somehow. I listened to their lyrics and imagined they were talking to me, teaching me about life and how I should be.

I had this crazy thought of wishing Steven Tyler was my dad. I had seen an interview where he talked about his past and how he was bullied as a kid, so I thought he would be perfect because he, too, had pain in his life and would probably understand me. I listened to his voice and saw how cool he was. Becoming his daughter would have been amazing.

Sometimes, I got lost in music, looking up at the sky and singing the song "Like a Prayer" by Madonna, wishing that whatever guardian was watching over me would hear me. That song held a lot of meaning for me when I was younger. I loved the words. My imagination became my reality. Going through a daily life of pain and suffering, I made it better with imagination. It's amazing how powerful a mind is when you are in survival mode.

After a while, my mother hired two nannies from Australia, named Ernie and Bert, to babysit us during the day while she was at work. They were tall, beautiful girls with very strong accents who loved shopping. I did not really understand most of what they said, but at least they were nice to us.

They once took us shopping at the mall, and we stopped to eat at Burger King in San Francisco, California. Pete and I were eating by this huge window, not talking, just staring through it. As I looked out, I saw people crossing the crosswalk, including a lady pushing her baby in a stroller and a man holding his coffee while walking.

All the taxis, cars, and buses were stopped, waiting for the light to turn green. We sat there staring down at the people. I was thinking about how small the people looked from up where we were, like ants.

Then the strangest thing happened! The people crossing the crosswalk and the cars all froze. They just stopped moving. Life stood still. I looked at Pete, and he looked at me as if to ask, "Are we both seeing this at the same time?" We then both looked back outside and saw that all the cars and people were back to normal. It felt like it was only a second or two when the world stopped. I am not sure what happened that day, but I will remember for the rest of my life.

Some people say it is impossible for something like that to happen. They say we just had an episode where we both were daydreaming about the same thing, or maybe it was a way out of the hell we were living, and both of us made it up and believed in our own imagination. My brother and I talk about that day to this day.

I think it is crazy how two people can see the same thing happen at the same time. I do not think I will ever know what happened that day. Not long after, Ernie and Burt quit their jobs as our nannies, and then I had to take responsibility and watch over Vanessa and Pete. I did not mind because I was in control of their safety and knew they were completely safe while I was in charge.

Vanessa was not exactly easy to take care of because it was so hard to get her to listen. If she were to tell our mom that I had grabbed her arm or was rough with her in any way, I would get a beating. This made things very difficult to get Vanessa to do what was right and stay in the house while my mom was out working.

There had been times when she would run to the street and lie there until I got her what she wanted. Vanessa was a bright girl who knew how to get things done her way, and that was by telling my mom, who she knew hated me and would hurt me if I did not do what she wanted. By then, she had won the upper hand, and I had no choice but to do things Vanessa's way.

It was a whole lot easier than having my mom beat me every time. Often, I did things with Vanessa that were fun and kept her busy so things would run smoothly for the day. I felt like a professional babysitter.

Chapter 4

Where Will Home Be Tomorrow?

My mom ended up dating a millionaire who was married with children. She waited for him to leave his wife, but it never happened. It was sad to see her wanting someone so badly that she became very depressed. My mother abandoned all her belongings and house to leave the city every three months or so. When she had these outbursts, she became very paranoid, and she did not want to be found. She grew extremely violent and psychotic, thinking people were out to get her.

I sometimes saw her peeking out the window as if someone was watching her. I would just sit there watching her look through the blinds and keep peeking out each window repeatedly, pacing back and forth, cracking her pinkie on her leg, and biting her nails. She always cracked her pinkie by hitting it on her leg when she was in deep thought. That's how I knew she was extremely thoughtful about something that she felt was a threat to her or had no control over. It was like she felt she was in danger, and she would go insane, pulling her hair out and yelling that she hated her life. I hated those moments. I wished I could take her pain away.

I did not want her to hurt herself anymore, and I was confused as to why she had these episodes. I had never seen my mom do drugs or anything that would make her like that; however, she did drink a box of Chardonnay every day.

My mother depended on Vanessa to keep her calm by hitting and yelling at her. It was so hard for a young girl to calm my mother down and feel the need to control her. Vanessa became abusive toward my mom over the years, hitting her and calling her names to get what she wanted from her and then acting like nothing had ever happened by the very next day. I was so sick of how dysfunctional their relationship was.

I had to sit on the toilet as my mom took her bath and told me her problems and all the things she wanted to do in life. Seeing she had positive dreams made me wish they would come true for her so she could be happy. I had to dye my mom's hair, making sure to put Vaseline on her forehead and ears to keep the dye off her skin. I wished I could be happy touching my own mother with love, but the truth was, I hated to touch her. It felt like a punishment to touch my own mother, and I blocked all my feelings about it.

Vanessa and I had to sleep in bed with our mom for years. She read all these tales and the Bible, and she talked about religion and her theory on it. I blocked it out, finding it hypocritical of her to talk about what was good but never practice what she preached. It made me angry that she wanted to do right by "God" but did the complete opposite.

I never let her manipulate me or brainwash me with what I knew was not right. I hated sleeping with them and turned my face toward the outside of the bed to breathe fresh air. Warm air made me feel like throwing up. The funny thing was, I never imagined myself escaping that life. At the time, I always thought that was just life.

I sometimes went swimming with Vanessa and pretended I was a mermaid and swam far into the ocean. I was trying to get away from the evil witch and live happily ever after! Though I never thought in real life I was going to get out of that hell, I pretended by using my imagination.

I lived in a lot of different houses and a lot of different lifestyles. My mom moved when business was slow or when she was mad at her boyfriend or her family members and did not want to be seen, so she would leave everything behind. When it got so bad, she really did not want to be found. We lived in shelters. One was at a church in San Francisco. The ladies who lived there were nuns who wore black and white. We had our own rooms. I shared a room with Pete; my mom and Vanessa had their own room. We ate three meals a day and had to get up and go to bed at the times they required. We got to choose an activity to learn, so I picked knitting.

One of the sisters taught me how to make a scarf. It was the coolest thing I had ever learned. They were all so nice, and I felt at home there. The best thing of all was that my mom was unable to hurt me there.

One night, Pete and I were sleeping on our bunk bed in our room. I was on the bottom, and he had the top bed. Pete whispered, "Jessica. Jessica, wake up." I was mad because I was tired and did not want to play. He said, "Look!" I looked around the room and saw twenty spirits walking around the room. They each had their own thing they were doing.

One had a book, another a ball. I asked Pete if he could see them. He said, "That's why I woke you up!"

I was not scared and did not have the urge to get out of bed and run. I just watched as I thought to myself that these people had so many different personalities. I wondered, "How am I not scared?" It was like I was dreaming, but I wasn't because Pete was seeing the same thing. I do not remember falling asleep, but I woke up in the morning, and they were not there anymore. I asked Pete what happened, and he said, "We just fell asleep, and they left." I could not believe we both saw the same thing.

Again, we both had seen something that could never be explained unless it was in our heads, and we made it up and believed our own imagination. I just can't see how two people could see the same thing at the same moment. To this day, we remember it and talk about what happened. We never told our mom because I did not want her to take my happiness from what I had seen away, so we kept it to ourselves.

My mom then found a place that was a three-bedroom trailer. There were a lot of drug addicts living in the trailer park. Pete and I had to take Vanessa to the park so my mom could bring her clients there. She worked and made good money but stopped working at the trailer because people kept getting into her business and asking what she did for a living. So she started to meet them at spas, at their houses, or in hotels. When she worked away from the house, we usually had to wait in the car, and that took at least an hour each time.

When my mom got frustrated and mad because the house was not clean enough or she did not make enough money to pay the rent or bills, she did her normal beating and threw me in the cold shower so I wouldn't bruise up. She kept yelling about how she hated me and asking why I wouldn't just die. I was crying, and my body was aching from the cold. Then she threw Comet cleaning powder all over me in the shower. I started to choke because I was breathing it in, and it was powdery. Then she poured bleach all over me, and breathing it in was so toxic. All I remember was not being able to breathe and feeling light-headed, and then I threw up all over the tub! She got me out and told me to clean it up. I slept in the tub that night while she went to sleep in a warm bed. I just wanted to die.

Soon it became summer, and my grandpa paid for me and Pete to attend summer camp. I was so happy because we got to go somewhere else that was fun for once. It was me and Pete on the bus full of kids looking at us like we were from space. We were very introverted and different, I guess. We did not put trust in or talk to many people. We stuck together, and having each other was all we needed at that time. Plus, I felt like an outcast due to my lifestyle and did not really feel capable of fitting in.

We got to camp in the woods, and it was so beautiful. We learned how to canoe, shoot a bow and arrow, swim, and enjoy many more amazing, fun activities. I met a girl who had attended the same camp a year before; she taught me how to eat my sausage and eggs by putting syrup over everything. I had never eaten syrup on my eggs and sausage before, and I must say it was pretty darn good. She taught me so many cool things about the camp. At night, the boys tried to sneak into the girls' cabin but got caught. They were watched by one of the camp teams, who were upset. It was exciting to almost get into trouble at camp. I forgot about my life at home after a few days of camp. I didn't ever want to go back home.

I went swimming one early morning with all the camp kids, and while I was in the water, a kid did a cannonball over me and hit me on the head. I passed out in the water and woke up to a hot lifeguard looking at me. He asked if I was okay, and I said my neck hurt and I felt dizzy. I was fine but had to wear a neck brace for a few days until the nurse said I could take it off. I had a crush on that lifeguard for the longest time.

I did not see Pete while I was in camp because they had us kids in different age groups. I did see him while we ate breakfast, lunch, and dinner. We learned so much about the forest, and they told us all kinds of funny and scary stories.

At the end of camp, we had a dance. I was so happy and did not want that feeling to end. I danced by myself and did not care what anyone thought. All I knew was I wanted to enjoy this moment and remember it for the rest of my life. We were packing our things the next morning, preparing to leave camp, and I was so sad.

As I sat looking out the window, I wondered why my life was so bad and why other kids got to live happily. They got to have great parents and a great night's sleep. I knew the abuse at home was not normal and knew my mother was wrong for what she was doing. What I didn't know was how I was going to break free without splitting up from Vanessa and Pete.

When we arrived home, my sister told us she had been held hostage at her babysitter's house. The babysitter's boyfriend had held the babysitter hostage with Vanessa, who was six years old at that time, in the trailer until the police busted the door down and took him into custody. The babysitter was a drug addict, and so was her boyfriend. I never knew why they held my sister hostage.

Vanessa had to learn to survive at an early age. She learned how to stay calm in bad situations that ended up taking control of my mom when she had her breakdowns. Vanessa had a lot on her shoulders for a child, and she dealt with our mom the only way she knew how. It was sad that she was very aggressive and felt the need to control my mom's behavior by hitting her and cursing at her.

My mom was happiest when her rich boyfriend took her out. Then she would come back after eating her favorite food and making money, have her wine, and make me sit on the toilet while she took a bath and told me about her day. She never asked how I was feeling; it was always about her and her only. I remember the way she splashed the water on her body and how her voice was so calm and so nice, like she would never hurt a fly. I hated seeing her naked, so I looked to the ground.

I never yelled at my mom or talked back and was never a problem child. I was always there to hear her out and protect Vanessa and Pete. Whenever she tried to hit them, I pushed them away and told my mom to go for me instead. She said I was just trying to be tough, and I thought I was the better one for doing that. I told her I didn't want her to take out her anger on them. I was so used to her hitting me that I knew how long it would take before she got tired and whom she was going to target first. Vanessa and Pete never told me that they were thankful for me trying to protect them, but I already knew they were.

My mom hit Pete when I could not stop her from doing so. Pete stood tall and just looked her in her eyes. She grew even madder and spit in his face. I almost vomited and looked away because I hated it. She told Pete she hated him and me because we came from a man she hated. She wished she never had us kids from him. She told us that we would never make it in life, we would never have kids, no one would take us in, and we were losers. She said we made her sick.

I felt so bad for Pete that he had to come home and get hit by her. We did nothing to her. When my mom hit me, Vanessa yelled, "Come on, Jessica, hit Mom back!" I told her to shut up.

My mom said, "Oh yeah, Jessica? You want to hit me?" I told her no.

Vanessa yelled, "Hit her! Do not let her hurt you no more!" I told her to shut up because she was making things worse. She was egging it on in a way. I never had the feeling of wanting to hit my mom. Somehow, I respected my mom and knew she had a problem.

I just wanted her to get all her frustration out on me so we all could go to bed and move on.

*****

One day, we all visited my aunt and slept over. Vanessa wanted a peanut butter and jelly sandwich. It was late, and everyone was sleeping. My aunt woke up to my mother in the kitchen and told her she could not make Vanessa a peanut butter and jelly sandwich. My aunt and my mom were arguing back and forth, and I heard my aunt telling my mom Vanessa was a spoiled brat.

My mom was so mad and woke us kids up and dragged us into the car. It was so late, and we were tired. But when my mom felt offended or rejected somehow, she didn't think about her actions or how she hurt people.

She was speeding down the street and saying she wanted to die and she wanted to kill all of us. We did not know how to stop her from crashing into innocent people or killing us all. Vanessa started hitting our mom and pulled her hair to get her to calm down and stop what she was doing. After that, our mom just kept driving and finally calmed down. She pulled over, and we slept in the car, with the windows fogged up and musty.

I woke up with my neck stiff and had totally forgotten that we were sleeping in the car. The sun started to come up, and I watched how darkness turned into sunlight in a matter of minutes. I had never seen anything more beautiful in my life. My mom took us for an egg muffin and her coffee. She was so calm and seemed so content with everything that had happened the night before. She acted like everything was normal and pretended nothing had happened.

My mom bought a black gun and said she wanted to kill my aunt. She even made out a plan on paper. My mom said she hated me most of all because I reminded her of my aunt, whom she hated. She felt my aunt took all her parents' attention. She kept her gun in a silver box and stored it in a locker at a special place. She always had all her mail sent to a PO box because she did not want anyone to know where she lived. I was so scared of her then because I realized she could really hurt someone.

I had to be extra nice to her and understanding so she would not do anything stupid. I cooked her favorite meals and gave her wine, which helped her feel like she was needed and understood. Wine made her calm. I also cleaned the house. From there, I knew how to make her calm.

My mom never did anything to my aunt but kept that plan in mind for years. I had good days when being extra nice and trying to prevent my mom from becoming angry worked for a while. On days when Vanessa made her mad or she did not make money, she hated life and blamed me for her life being so bad. As soon as my mom targeted me, my sister would get in the middle and tell her to stop, which made her even more mad. My mom and Vanessa had a bond, and if my mom felt she was protecting me or taking my side somehow, she hated me even more than ever. She would hit herself and pull her hair out.

My sister had to calm her down. Calming her down my sister's way meant slapping my mom, pulling her hair, yelling at her, and calling her names. It almost looked like what my mom did to me. Vanessa would scream at my mom, "See how it feels? This is what Jessica feels!"

Vanessa had enough of my mom's outburst and got up on the table, holding a phone with a cord attached. My sister was swinging it like she was going to rope a cow. She was screaming, "Come closer, Mom! Try to hit me now!" She swung the phone toward my mom and hit the front of her head with it. My mom yelled, "Ouch!" Vanessa told her that she was going to keep hitting her if she didn't calm down. I had to get Vanessa to stop.

My mom went to the bathroom and was crying, and for some reason, I felt so bad for her and asked if she was okay. Then I got ice for her head. Vanessa felt bad afterward too. Mom's forehead was swelling up fast, and she was sick for a week with a headache. She looked as if she was growing a single horn in the middle of her forehead.

After Vanessa calmed her down, my mom would act like nothing had happened and tell my sister she loved her and bought her everything she wanted. Vanessa quickly learned how to manipulate her and get what she wanted. From there on, Vanessa developed an extremely aggressive, blackmailing, and manipulative behavior, starting to act like my mom and learning how to overpower my mom.

Vanessa would never let her do to her what Mom was doing to me. Vanessa said she had to do what she did to my mom to avoid getting hit or controlled by my mom, and she said I should do the same. I would never do something like that. My sister was taking care of herself by then, and I did not worry about her as much.

I used to take Vanessa to figure skating class on the weekends. She had gone to many activities. I was like her mother. I took care of her and tried to teach her good things. I wanted her to be a good person. Vanessa was very bossy toward me when she wanted her way but never disrespected me like she did my mom.

One day, my mom had to move to San Francisco with another aunt of mine. She was happy because she had work there, and that's why we ended up living in her house. My mom left her belongings in her garage. We stayed for about a month, and I was happy because my cousins gave me their hand-me-downs. They had a huge bathroom, where they had this vintage bathtub with tiger feet. It was so deep, and I loved to feel as if I was swimming. San Francisco homes were very different from the ones I was used to living in.

I had brought all our animals, in cages, to her house. We had guinea pigs, big rats, birds, and hamsters. Vanessa and my mom loved animals as much as me—at least we had one thing in common. I had put them all in a room and closed the door.

The next day, my cousins found a stray dog. It was so cute, and he had no collar, but he was hungry. My cousins wanted to keep him, so they put him in the backyard. We were playing outside and did not see the dog, so I went to look in the house. I looked from room to room and saw the door to the room where I had left the animals cracked open. My heart was beating so fast in fear of what I was going to see. As I walked up to the door, I heard the chomping and smacking of a large animal. I opened the door and saw the dog sticking his face into one of the cages where we kept the rats. I looked around the room and found all the animals chewed up and tossed all over the floor.

Their bodies were lifeless, their legs still twitching and their eyes glossy. I screamed, "Help!" I grabbed the dog and pushed him out the door and closed it. I went to check and see if I could save one of the animals. It smelled like wet animals in the room. The stench of the dog's saliva stunk up the whole room. I was gagging and crying at the same time, not able to believe the dog would do such a thing. He did not eat them, just chewed them up. He crushed their bones and mangled their bodies and went to the next one. I sat there waiting for their bodies to stop twitching and die or get better before I decided to put them in a garbage bag.

In the end, they were all dead. My cousins called the dogcatchers to pick the dog up, and I hated him so badly for killing my animals. Vanessa was so upset. I watched as the dog was being put in the truck with no worries on his face, and I was so mad that he had no idea what he had done. It was almost as if he was proud of it. I watched the van as it drove away, thinking this must be a dream. Then I went back to clean up the mess he'd left. I remember that smell to this day.

One day, my mom and my aunt got into a huge fight. My aunt said my mom owed her because we had stayed for a couple of months. My mother was so mad and told us to get in the car. As she drove off, my aunt yelled out, "You're not getting your things back!" I was so scared of what my mom was going to do next. She drove so fast down streets while people were crossing them and cars were going in opposite directions. I remember her yelling out, "I hate you, Jessica! You messed up my life, and now we don't have anywhere to live because of you!" I wanted to open the car door and jump out. My mom had to be stopped. Vanessa was sitting in the passenger seat, yelling at my mom to stop. Then she pulled my mom's hair and slapped her in her face.

My mom was not slowing down. Vanessa was yelling, "Mom, you're going to kill us!" My sister kept pulling her hair and slapping her. Finally, my mom pulled over. We were all so scared. My mom was hitting her head on the steering wheel, yelling, and screaming.

People just walked by like nothing was happening. I do not understand how people could see a car full of kids and just ignore her driving crazy and pulling over, yelling, and hitting herself. I wished she would have gotten caught.

Vanessa said in a soft voice, "Are you okay? Mom, I love you." To me, it was sick for my sister to give her that kind of attention, but I knew it was the only way for her to stop. Pete did nothing, like always. He was the oldest of us kids. I always wished for him to protect us, and he never did. He always detached himself emotionally, as if he were not even there in reality when all of this was going on.

My mom calmed down and sat there thinking of where to go. As we sat in the quiet car, all I could hear was her chewing her nails as she stared out the window. I was waiting for the next crazy thing she was going to do. Vanessa told her she was tired and wanted to go somewhere to sleep. My mom said, "Fine, I am going to call my boyfriend and tell him what is going on," and then she rented a hotel for a week.

My mom met up with her boyfriend, and he got her a condo. My mom had a lot of business there and started to make money. We had it pretty good because she stayed out all day and sometimes night. The best part was when she came home happy. You know business doesn't always go well all the time. Well, for her, it was getting slow. She had more time on her hands to be home. I did not like it because that meant she would get agitated, and her being agitated meant more beatings. One time, she was late for an appointment, and I was trying to make the room spotless and wanted to clean the TV. I was spraying Windex on it, and my mom kicked me with the tip of her high heel. She kicked my tailbone and said, "That's enough!" I could not breathe. It hurt so badly. My mom did not know how badly I was hurt. I think she broke my tailbone, and it hurt for six months.

Chapter 5

Just over the Bridge

I was once picked up early from school because my mom had no work, so it made her think of my stepdad. I knew something was going to happen. She told me that I had no idea how she hated me. She closed all the blinds and curtains. I was so scared because my sister and brother were not there to at least save me if she got out of control. She went on and on about how my stepdad loved to touch me more than her, saying I was a slut for trying to steal her husband from her. She said she hated me because he went to jail because of me.

She beat me badly that day. She ripped my hair out of my head. She held me on the ground and sat on my chest with my hands at my side, making sure I could not block my face. She said, "Look at me when I am talking to you!" She slammed my head on the ground so hard, many times, and then pulled my lips. I felt my bottom lip ripping, and I tasted blood. She was looking me in my eyes, and I kept trying to look away while she was "ripping my face off." I looked into her eyes. It was the scariest thing because I saw no soul. She looked like she was not all there; it was like she had blacked out and was beating me and not knowing it. She had not one ounce of remorse for what she was doing.

She then started jabbing her thumbs into my eyes. I screamed, and she choked me until my eyes seemed to pop out of their sockets. They felt like they were cracking and burning inside. I don't know how to explain it, but it was the scariest feeling ever.

As she was choking me, I could not see anymore, and I was thinking, "So this is how I'm going to die?" I wished for her to just kill me. She ran out of breath and stopped. She yelled out, "I hate you!" My vision was blurry. I pretended to be passed out, hoping for her not to hit me anymore. I have so many memories, but those eyes of hers when she was beating me can never go away. I do not know how she did not get tired of beating me, but it was not over yet. She spit on my face—not just any spit but a loogie.

When she spit on my face, it usually meant she was done. Well, not this time. This time was different. She peeked outside and looked through every window. As I lay on the floor where she left me, I wondered what she was planning. I was scared to move and wipe off her spit. I could smell her spit on my face, and I wanted to throw up.

I kept focusing on what she was doing. I did not want to make her madder than she already was, so I stayed calm. She had gone to the other room and gotten a chain for hanging plants with. She kept talking about how she hated me and how my real dad was a loser. She said I reminded her of her sister she hated. She whipped me with that chain so hard, over and over. I passed out and woke up to see her still beating me. I was so numb and tired and felt like throwing up. My mom told me to get in the shower. I hurt so badly all over.

Vanessa and Pete came home from school and asked me what happened. I told them I did not know. She took me out of school, and she was mad. I had to stay home for two and a half months. My mom lied to the school and said I was visiting my "father." I had to recover from what she had done to me. I honestly think she was not as stupid or insane as people thought. She planned things out and knew how to cover her tracks. She always acted as if she was the victim.

Pete and I wanted to run away from home. We joked about it all the time. We said that we would travel the world. I had these dreams where I would fly over the ocean and go to another world. When I was flying, it felt so good. I felt free and did not want to wake up. I was so angry when I had to be awake in this reality.

One day, Pete said we should run away when my mom left for work. Vanessa was at her friend's house for the weekend, and it would be perfect. I told my brother we had no money. He told me not to worry because he had gotten money from my mom's stash in her room, where she had eighty dollars. That day, we packed our backpacks full of clothes and walked to find jobs.

All the managers and the restaurants were asking where our parents were. One lady told us to stay where we were, and we thought to ourselves that she was calling the police. We ran so fast out of there and went to the mall, where my brother bought a Darth Vader sword that lit up and made sound effects. He said it would protect us from harm.

We decided to walk over the main bridge to another city. This bridge was as long as the Golden Gate Bridge. It was very windy and dark outside. As we walked over, I could hear the ocean water swishing and feel the breeze on my face. My lips were chapped because we had no water to drink, and the wind was blowing at me. My brother and I thought that just over the bridge was a new life where we would be free.

As the cars drove by fast, the bridge felt like it was bouncing up and down. It was dark, and I could not see the water or anything but where I was walking. I heard a siren and saw the lights of a police car. The policeman told us to stop and put our hands on our heads. Pete said, "We almost made it." The policeman got out of his car and asked us where we were going. We told him over the bridge. He said our mom was worried sick about us. He said for us to get in the car, and he would drive us home.

On our way there, he asked why we were running away, but we did not say a word. We finally got to our house. My mom opened the door and looked happy to see us. She was never that happy to see us, and I wish I had told the policeman the truth. When he left, Pete and I had to stand in the corner. My mom had called my grandpa and told him we were troublemakers and ran away from home. My mom acted like she was a victim of having bad children when we were the ones who were suffering at the hands of our mother.

One summer day, Pete and I were playing on our bikes, and we invented this game where we would ride our bikes toward each other, and whoever turned first was a chicken. There I was, ready for the okay to go, focusing on Pete on his bike. Pete said, "Go!" I went fast as I could because all I knew was I had to win. I woke up lying on the ground with Pete asking me if I was okay. I did not remember crashing at all. I got up and tried to act like nothing had happened like I was fine.

I looked at my arm and noticed it was broken. I was so in shock that it did not hurt or even feel broken, just twisted up. I thought of my mom and told Pete that I could not tell her about my arm being broken or she would kill me. Pete said we must tell her so we could get my arm fixed, so I went home and told my mom about how I broke my arm, and sure enough, she was so mad. She was so angry while she drove to the hospital.

I sat there at that doctor's table, so disappointed in myself because I wished I was not such a burden on my mom. I wished I had not broken my arm and had done everything right at home. A song I liked came on the radio, and I sang the lyrics to myself. I just wanted to be in my own world so I would feel the pain and worry. When we got to the hospital, the doctor came in to ask how I broke my arm, and I told him. He ended up stretching my arm back into place. I heard it pop, and then he started to wrap it in a cast. The doctor said that I had to wear the cast for two and a half months. I thought to myself, *There goes my summer. Mom will use this to ruin my whole summer.*

Pete then started to keep a knife under his bed. He was so used to my mom waking one of us up by grabbing us by our hair and beating us till she was out of breath. I think it was a way of being able to sleep better at night. She found out about the knife and called my grandpa. She said that Pete had a knife under his mattress and that she was scared for her life. In reality, it could have been that Pete had gotten sick of my mom beating him and was the one who was afraid for his life.

When my mom told my grandpa, he told my mom to put him in a boys' home, so she did. I did not see Pete for a year; in that year, it was the same hate from mom. Life continued as it was, and my mother was relentless in her abuse. Her mental illness was getting worse than before. Having others look at me and Pete as bad kids became a normal way of life, and we did not really care what they thought. Only we were the ones who knew the truth, and that was all that mattered. I was counting the years until I turned eighteen and had much hope as the days went on. I survived another day, and it was one step closer to freedom.

I often thought of what I would do when I could make my own choices. I thought of having a family and being in love. I thought of what I would look like, what style I would have, and what kind of car I would drive. I had hope, and hope was very helpful in times like these. I was so happy Pete ended up moving back home with us. I heard all kinds of stories about how it was in the boys' home.

It sounded so fun. I was so happy he got to be himself, and that was good. I wished he was not back in the hellhole we lived in, but at the same time, I was happy he was back. It was a bittersweet situation.

My mom was practicing a new form of spirituality. She said if we all wished for the same thing and drew it on paper, then it would come true. We all drew a two-story house with a white picket fence on a large piece of land. My mom's boyfriend had a nice ranch home in Dixon, California, that was very similar to the one we wished for. He ended up letting us live in his home because it was vacant. We all moved into a house exactly like the one we had drawn. I don't know whether it was a coincidence or if our wish came true.

As we arrived at our new home, we all climbed out of the car, and I just stood there looking at a home that I never thought I would ever live in. It was in the country and was a two-story with a basement and attic. The basement had wine stashed in it, very old wine. The attic had some old things in there as well. The house had five rooms, including a big kitchen and a family room. Outside, it was beautiful, with a white patio that wrapped all around the house. It had one orange tree that smelled so good when it bloomed. There were grape vines that had big purple grapes. It also had this olive tree that made a mess of black olives on the ground, and I hated to step on them because they stained my shoes. I did not like it very much. In the back of the house was an old barn where an old white owl lived. She was so pretty. She left pellets on the ground, and I would cut them open and try to build whatever she had eaten. Most of them were small mice.

The house was old, and when we walked into the living room, the floor made a squeaking sound. It had a smell of old dusty wood. I really liked that house. It was peaceful, and I had fun catching animals there.

Snakes were my favorite reptile. I caught them but then let them go. One time, I left one in a box because someone had run over its tail, and I was going to heal it. When I woke up in the morning, it was not in the box. I was scared that my mom would find out. I looked all over that house and could not find it. There were old heating vents that it could have gone through. After a week of looking, I stopped and never found it.

I remember it was raining so hard that it was flooding the basement. I went down into the basement to check it. I saw something I had never seen before: little mice jumping and trying not to drown. I mean hundreds of mice. They were all squeaking and crawling over each other to breathe air. I had to do something, so I got a bucket. I started to scoop them up and throw them into the bucket. They were all so wet! I was overwhelmed with fear of one drowning.

I could not sleep that night, thinking of those mice, like I could have done more to save all of them. Then I worried I might catch a disease from all those mice, so I tried to block my thoughts and go to sleep. The next morning, I woke up, and it had stopped raining. I dumped out the mice I did save, but some were dead. I guess from being packed in with so many mice, they had a heart attack or went into shock. Most of them ran away. I put the dead mice in the barn, thinking the old white owl would eat them. I went to check on them the next day, and they were still there, and so was the owl. I guess owls don't like dead food.

*****

I started middle school, and it was weird to see boys dressed as "cowboys." I had never seen boys or girls dressed like that. They called themselves "hicks." But I made a friend, and we hung out all the time at school.

My mom was still doing the same escort business, going to work in another city most of the time at men's houses or hotels, which gave me time to come home from school to clean up and make dinner. She came home when we were all in bed, but I slept with one eye open to be prepared for what my mom was going to do next.

I prayed that the house was clean enough and things had gone well at work as I heard her car coming into the driveway. My heart started beating so fast, and I felt all tingly inside. I heard the key being put into the doorknob and then felt my body shutting down and turning numb. I was scared for her to find something wrong.

As she walked around the house, I wanted to hide and for her to never find me. At the same time, I wanted to jump out of bed to tell her to go ahead and just kick my ass and get it over with so I could sleep. I couldn't sleep without knowing what she was planning to do to me. She jumped me out of nowhere a lot of times and had her days when she would find something and days when she would beat me so badly again when I had to take cold showers and not go to school until the bruises healed. She knew where to hit so it would not show. My mom had a mental illness going on, but she was not stupid.

My mom ended up with an opportunity to get more business where it was legal to be in the escort business in Nevada. She left us kids at the house and put me in charge of things, first making sure there was food and things we needed to take care of ourselves. I took Vanessa to her elementary school, and Pete and I went to middle school. We walked home, and I made TV dinners that my mom had left for us in the freezer. She was gone for two months, and life was so good.

My mom sent us money in the mail. I had Pete get food from the store on his bicycle. I loved making dinner. Pete and I would make up different dishes, and Vanessa loved them.

Things were quiet, and then one day, I told my friend that we had been alone for a couple of months and that my mom was in Nevada working. She told a friend of hers, and somehow someone told a teacher, and then that teacher told the police. When we were walking home, we looked across the cornfield and saw a bunch of flickering lights all around our house. As we walked closer and closer to the house, I knew those were cops all around our house. They had guns pointed at the house, and as I got closer, a police officer saw me and told me to stay back. I asked him why they were there.

We told them we lived there. They all came toward us and asked if we were okay. We said yes and asked why they were there. They said that someone had told them we were alone and our mom was out of state. We said yes, our mom was away. They came into the house and looked all over. They looked in our drawers, rooms, closets, cabinets, and refrigerator. They said the fridge was full of food, and that was important. They said we had to have an adult to take care of us. They asked if we had a friend who could take care of us until our mom came back. I could only think of one, and that friend saved us from having my mom come back home.

We went to school normally every day, and then three months went by. One day, I was mopping the kitchen floor when I asked Pete to hurry up and help me clean the house. Pete was busy playing around and had run to the kitchen, yelling, "Bruce Lee!" looking like he was karate kicking me as a joke and slipped. He yelled out, "My knee, my knee!" I told Pete to stop playing around, and I was going to bed. Pete continued to cry, and I began to worry. He was telling the truth and, in fact, was seriously hurt.

I went back to the kitchen and turned on the light to see Pete looking pale and sweating. He said he had broken his knee, and sure enough, his kneecap was up to his thigh. I did not know what to do. I ran to the ranch behind the house, and no one was there, so I went to the next ranch that was close by and told them what had happened.

They told me to call 911 and they would send an ambulance. All I could think about was that we were going to get into so much trouble. How was I going to tell our mom? I was thinking of excuses but could not come up with one or hide this problem.

The ambulance showed up and said he needed to go to the hospital, so I got my sister and headed to the ambulance to go with Pete. I gave the number to call my mom and told her that Pete needed to have surgery, and an adult had to be there to sign paperwork and stay with us kids. My mom came back home.

She was a different person; she came home even madder than when she had left. Pete ended up having knee surgery and had metal plates and rods to hold his kneecap in place. He had to wear a cast for three months and then a knee brace for another three months with therapy. I never thought Pete would ever break a bone in his body. He was not a kid who got hurt all the time. I felt so bad for him because I knew how it felt to break a bone, but his was much worse.

After a few months, my ears were in pain and progressed to infection. I knew if I asked my mom, she would get mad that she had to take me to the doctor. When my ears grew even more infected, I could not hear her well—I could only see her lips moving. Even when flushing the toilet, I could not hear a thing.

It was so painful for my ears to pop. I asked my mom to please take me to the doctor. She said I should suffer with my pain for messing up her life. Finally, we had to go to school, and she did not want people to question her, so she took me to the doctor. I got some medicine, and I was so thankful. I wanted to tell my mom, "Thank you," but I just kept it in.

My mother was still an escort, but this time she had gone to work in another city at clients' houses, and she booked hotels at night, so she was gone most of the time now. Her new work schedule gave me time to get home from school, clean, and make dinner for Vanessa and Pete.

Still I said the same prayer to myself every night, praying that the house was clean enough if she did come home, that everything went well at the office, and that she was not fixated on the memory of perverted Earl. I continued to sleep with one eye open, preparing myself for my mother's next move.

I never talked back to, yelled at, or hit my mother. I never had the feeling of wanting to hit her. I respected her because she gave me life and she was my mother. I did not like hitting people in general, and it got to the point where her abuse meant nothing to me because I was so numb from it emotionally and physically. I knew she had problems. I was told my mom had been raped and neglected as a child, and I felt sorry for her and tried hard not to take what she said and did to me as hard.

Pete never told my mother to stop when she was abusing me, but I always protected him. I did not mind taking the brunt of my mother's anger for him because I never wanted Vanessa or Pete hurt by her and thought I could handle the abuse better than them. She belittled me when I did that, telling me I was just trying to act tough.

When I couldn't stop her and my mother hit Pete, he just stood tall and stared her down in the eyes. It made her even angrier, so she spit in his face and screamed that she hated us both because we came from the man she hated. She screamed at him that he was going to be just like our father, a loser and a drunk.

I felt so bad for him. It didn't matter how regular this way of life was for us; it was still hard to watch. I hated it. Pete and I were nothing to her. We made her sick. She told us constantly that we'd never be successful in life.

My mom ended up having a nervous breakdown and left the place we were living in. She got into a fight with her married boyfriend, who owned that house where we were living rent-free. She did not want him to find her again, as with everyone she got into an argument with. We had to sleep in an RV camping ground. She pitched a tent, and we slept there for five months.

We showered in these bathrooms with no walls to keep everyone from seeing each other naked. It got hard to go to school because our clothes were dirty, and we all looked so tired. We couldn't sleep or rest when we did not know what she was planning from one minute to the next. She was like a ticking time bomb. She decided to move to Winnemucca, Nevada. On our way there, she found a dog and kept it.

She was driving a van with seats that turned into a bed. It was me, Pete, Vanessa, my mom, and a dog, and this dog had worms. As I lay down to sleep, the dog kept putting his butt in my face, so I had to look at his butthole, which is how I saw these tiny white worms wiggling out of his butt. They were all over the blankets, and I felt so sick and dirty. I could not sleep. All I could think about was if these worms could get up my nose and ears or go through my skin.

One day, I was in the car while my mom was in the store. I decided to let the dog out of the car, hoping it would run away. It did not run away, and it made me so mad. Sleeping with that dog was so horrible! I just kept finding worms all over the car seat. Finally, on our way to Carson City, Nevada, my mom dropped the dog off at an animal shelter. She put him in a cage where they allowed drop-offs any time of day. It was so nice finally living without worms.

I kept an eye out for them in the car because it still had that dog smell. I hated being in that car. I do not know why she did this to us. She was smart and able to work, yet she chose to make us live through all that because she wanted to. She was so focused on not wanting anyone to find her that she did not think of our well-being. She just felt we were at fault for her life being a mess.

One day, she went to an appointment in this building. I realized we were in Winnemucca, and we stayed at this weird house where mothers could stay until they were able to get on their feet. We had to go to bed and eat when they said. I wished it was like the one we stayed at in San Francisco. I loved it there because they were clean and taught good things, and most of all, they had good food. This place was dirty and just weird. I was always scared to sleep.

We stayed for a couple of weeks. Then my mom went to a man's trailer, and I was so scared to be there. It was a very small trailer, and this guy was telling my mom he did not like kids. My mom said that we would not bother him. We stayed in the living room of the trailer, and my mom and this man slept together in his tiny room. It was strange because we did not know this man. I did not know if she was going to allow him to molest us kids. I stayed alert to what was said, and I watched his body language. It was very quiet, and he bossed my mom around a lot. She did everything he said. I didn't know if we were being held hostage or if she was willing to get treated this way. With my mom, anything was possible.

Vanessa, Pete, and I went out to play a lot. We climbed this big mountain across from the trailer park, and it was snowing and cold. We did not care because it was better than staying in the small trailer. We got lost up in the mountain and did not know how to get back home. It took so long just to get back to where we could see a road.

We finally found one after dark and followed the road back home. My mom and the guy we lived with were fighting. He was screaming at her and saying he did not want her in the business she was in. She said he could not tell her what to do. He said that we had to leave his trailer by morning.

My mom was so angry and told me to get in the car, so I did. She was in the trailer for a while. I did not know if she wanted me to sleep in the car or if she was coming back out. Soon she came out of the trailer and hopped in the car. She closed the car door and just sat there. She told me in a soft voice, "I don't know what the fuck to do." She started the car, and I wondered why she was leaving Vanessa and Pete.

She drove up this hill and told me she wished I was dead so I would not cause her any more problems. She went to this hill and parked the car. I was wondering what she was going to do. She told me to get out of the car and started to yell at me and push me. I noticed something in her hand: a knife.

I went into a rage and said, "What? You're going to kill me?" She said that she should get rid of me for good. I got crazy and took off my clothes. The ground was full of snow, and it was so cold, but I did not care about that at the time. I yelled out, "Okay, kill me! Come on! You're doing it every day anyway! Just get it over with!" I started to pull out my hair. I scratched my face and was going insane.

As I stood there naked, my mom just looked surprised and said, "You're crazy! What the hell is wrong with you?"

I yelled out, "Kill me!" I begged, "Please, I don't want to be here anymore!"

My mom said that I had gone crazy, and she did not know why. She told me to put my clothes on and get in the car. While I was putting my clothes back on, I was thinking, "What the hell just happened?" All I had to do was act crazy for her to leave me alone. I hated feeling that way and never acted like her ever again. I felt ugly and out of control with my emotions.

From there, we moved to Carson City, Nevada. We stayed at another small shelter. They gave her a car to drive around and look for work and a place of our own. The car broke down as soon as we got it, but they said they could not fix it. We had no food during the day, so my mom made up some plan where the three of us kids had to separate and ask for money from people walking out of the stores. We later met up at the car and counted all the money we had made. I was the one who always brought in the most money. My mom finally got a place of her own, a motel room that she paid for daily.

I remember her leaving a couple of dollars on the counter for food every morning. We had a microwave and a small cooler, so we had to get ice every day. We bought things like cereal, milk, bologna, bread, mayo, cheese, and some lettuce to make sandwiches. We ate cereal in the morning. One of those mornings, we were eating cereal that we had bought from the corner dollar store.

As I was eating it, I looked into the bowl and saw something wiggling in the milk. I scooped it up with my spoon; it was a mealworm. There were so many of them in my bowl. I realized I had eaten a few before I noticed them. I spit out my cereal and felt so grossed out. I never ate that cereal again. To this day, I always look at the cereal to make sure it is fresh and wormless.

After my mother got tired of trying to make money in that city, she moved to Reno, Nevada. My brother and I went to school there for a couple of months. When we got there, the principal had a talk with us in his office. He said he did not like Californians coming to his school and causing trouble. If we were to cause trouble, then we would be kicked out. I do not see how we were a threat. We were just two kids in middle school who looked like bums. We always looked tired; I slept in the back of the class every period.

I wore a hooded sweater to cover my face during class so the teacher would not see me sleep. Sitting way far in the back of the class made it easier to get away with that. I was glad I could at least sleep safely in school because I could not sleep in peace at home.

We got out of school one day, and my mom had all her belongings in the car. As we climbed into the car, she said we were going back to California. She said she had an idea to rent an apartment in Dixon, the same town we had just left. I hoped we would move back to the ranch home, but it was good just to be able to go back to California, where at least I knew some people.

Chapter 6

My First Boyfriend

We moved into our apartment and started going back to school, where I saw people I knew from middle school. A few months passed, and I had my first boyfriend when I was thirteen years old. It was the first time anyone had ever really paid attention to me. The way he looked at me made me feel wanted; he was so nice to me. It felt like I was really living for once, and I felt happy for the first time in a long time. I finally had something in life to look forward to. I had my fourteenth birthday, and my boyfriend wanted me to go to his car and hang out.

He ended up making out with me and unzipped his pants and asked me to perform oral sex on him. I had never done anything like that before, and as I went down on him, I vomited all over him and his car before I could do anything. I ran out of the car and was so embarrassed. He called me and said it was okay and we could try another day. I was not looking forward to it at all.

My boyfriend had a birthday party when he turned seventeen. He invited me up to his room to look at his new radio that night. When I went upstairs, he closed the door behind him, which made me nervous. I wanted to go back downstairs, but he told me to relax and sit on the bed.

I tried talking to him for a while about music, but he kept kissing me and trying to take off my clothes. He became aggressive when I started to get up because he wanted to have sex. I didn't want to. I told him I wasn't ready and wanted to get married first. He sat on the bed and laughed at me. I thought to myself that maybe I was asking for too much.

I felt like I had asked for this in a way because I came to his party and went up to his room. I finally did what he wanted, so he turned up the radio and put on a condom. I couldn't believe he had planned this all along. My dreams of getting married first were out the door, and my heart was beating so fast that I wanted to pass out. He was the first person who ever showed me affection of any kind, so I didn't want to disappoint him, and I didn't want to lose him. After he was finished, he told me to get dressed and left the room, closing the door behind him. I felt so dirty and so used. He did not say he loved me or hold me afterward. He didn't care. I went to the bathroom to clean myself up because I was bleeding.

I wobbled like a duck when I walked around afterward, and my boyfriend was nowhere to be found. As I was searching, I felt as if everyone was staring at me, like they knew I had just lost my virginity. Not long after that, I gave up and went home.

He called me later and told me I needed to buy him new sheets because I had gotten blood all over his set. I was so mad and embarrassed at the same time, and there was no one I could talk to about what had happened. I had no family that would listen to me and no real friends to confide in. I was so alone.

The next day at school, I found him with a group of his friends. I was nervous because it would be the first time we saw each other since having sex. When I saw him, they were all laughing. Then they looked at me standing there and started cracking up even harder. He had tape-recorded me when we were having sex. I started crying and begging him to stop playing that, to please get rid of it.

He told me he didn't want me anymore, so I walked away, and everyone in the halls started laughing at me. I hated having to see him in school after that. He was a jerk and made me feel so used.

*****

Pete had moved to his friend's house, and I was so upset that he had left me once again and did not care if I was going to be okay. One night, my mom was talking to Vanessa about how she thought I'd messed up her life and how Earl preferred me over her. She kept drilling Vanessa until she was fed up and stressed from her constant negative talk and from my mom trying her hardest to brainwash her into believing it was true.

Vanessa was mad and told my mom to stop telling her those things, saying my mom was crazy and sick to be talking like that and believing her own thoughts. My mom yelled out, "Oh yeah! Is that what you think? Why are you protecting her? Jessica was the one who ruined our lives. If it wasn't for her, we would be happy." As I lay there wondering why I was alive and feeling like a burden on my mom, I wished I were dead. I went to bed, and I could still hear my mom going on and on and on about the same subject. It was about my stepdad, as my mom tried to brainwash my sister.

Vanessa was crying and begging my mom to stop. My heart was beating fast, and I felt like throwing up. I was so angry and fed up from hearing it all that I got up out of bed and went to her room. I saw Vanessa in the corner of the room, with her hands covering her ears. She was crying hard. I told my mom to leave her alone because it had nothing to do with her, and she should talk to me about it.

My sister said, "Jessica, don't make it worse!"

My mom said, "I hate you! I want to get rid of you!" She told me to get out of her face, so I did.

I went to bed but did not sleep; instead, I lay there thinking of what she was going to do next. I could hear Vanessa calming my mom down. My sister was ten years old at that time. She felt she had to be responsible for making peace in the home. She was the only one who could calm my mom down. I lay in bed so scared of what was next, but I kept falling asleep. My eyes and body felt heavy.

I was mad at myself that I kept falling asleep. I closed my eyes, thinking I was going to keep my mind awake so I could hear her coming down the hall. I felt hot and cold flashes with sharp, stabbing pains in my body. My nerves were shot, and I was so scared of what she was going to do to me.

She grabbed me by my hair and dragged me out of bed. I started to block my stomach so she would not punch it like she always did. She said, "Don't worry. I am not going to kick your ass. I won't waste my time. I am going to drop you off where I heard a little girl was raped and thrown in a ditch."

I was so scared! My mom told me to get in the car. My sister was sleeping, and my mom carried her to the car. My mom had the car running and warmed up. She had planned it all, and she wanted my sister to be warm in the car. My sister asked my mom where we were going. My mom told her we were going for a ride. She was sleepy, and it was so quiet in the car.

All I could hear was the heater air flowing through the vents. My mom was biting her nails and spitting them out. I wondered what time it was, so I glanced at the clock on the car radio—one fifty-six in the morning. I could not believe this was happening. As my mom drove over a bridge, I paid close attention to where we were going. We drove for an hour, and she told me that truckers went through there all the time. The place where she was dropping me off was in the country, with no streetlights and few cars driving by. It looked dead outside.

My mom pulled over and told me to get out. I looked outside and just wanted to talk to her and apologize to her that I had messed up her life. But I did not want to because I would be lying to her, and she would never believe it if I did. As I got out, my sister cried and asked my mom why she was doing this. My mom said, "This way, you and I can live happy."

I got out and closed the door. She did not think twice and drove off. I did not know where I was. It was dark and cold. I watched her brake lights in the pitch dark getting smaller the farther she drove away. I followed in the direction my mom drove.

As I walked, I kept tripping in the ditch where the water ran for the cornfield. I tried to stay on the road, but it was so dark. When you can't see at all, it is so hard to stay straight when you are walking. I got better at feeling my way around. I kept walking and had this feeling of wanting to scream. All I could hear were crickets and birds peeping. I couldn't see, not even my hand. It was like I was blind.

Out in the country, there were no streetlights, making it so hard to see a thing, so I tried to use my senses and stay calm. I was thinking of what my mom had said about a trucker picking me up and raping me. I thought if I screamed, it might bring someone who would do just that. So I stayed quiet and knew, in a matter of hours, it would be sunrise.

I walked and walked and looked forward until I saw a speck of light far into the distance. I kept walking toward it. It was the only thing I could see, as if in 3D, because it was the only thing shining out from the darkness. My focus was only on making it toward that light in the distance. As I walked, I could hear my breathing, and my breathing made it shaky.

I was shaking from head to toe and thought I was going insane with fear. I just focused on my breathing and the way it sounded when I walked. I tried breathing slowly and smoothly, telling myself it was going to be okay. At the same time, I could not believe what was happening. I thought I was dreaming and it was all going to be over when I woke up.

My feet were hurting, and my body was thumping as my blood circulated all over. As I drew closer to the light, I noticed the walnut trees in the field and thought to myself, *I can see now!* I was happy, but the only bad part was, if I could see, it meant people who drove by could see me too. I walked even faster to get back to the city. I crossed a cornfield and went through a field of walnut trees toward that small light I had seen.

As the sun came up, that little light I followed grew dimmer. I realized where I was and figured out how to get home from there. When I reached town, I finally found out that the light that had guided me home was a Denny's restaurant. I felt everyone was staring at me. Maybe it was all in my head.

As I came closer to the apartments, I felt sick, not wanting to show my face back at the house. But I did not have anywhere to go, and all I wanted to do was sleep. When I got to the stairs of the front door, my mom opened the door and was laughing at something my sister had said. She saw me standing there, and I did not say one word. She told me to get in the house and get ready for school. I got ready and went to school at seven forty-five in the morning. I entered the school and wondered if people could tell that I had been walking for hours in the dark.

I started to hate hearing people's conversations because all they would complain about was the latest style they were going to the mall for, how a girl's friend was talking to her boyfriend, or even what their parents made them eat for dinner the night before. I hated that! At least they had normal lives, where I wanted to be. I was sick of being alone and abused.

Chapter 7

Trip to Juvenile Hall

I made a friend not too long after that, and her name was Kiana. She invited me to hang out with her after school one day, and she happened to live in the same complex as me. We eventually became best friends, and her mom was nice. I went there as often as I could.

I decided I didn't want to go back home, and Kiana told me she had some friends with an apartment there at the complex where I could stay. The apartment was an all-male roommate environment, and they let me sleep on the couch for the night. I never told my mother I wasn't coming home; I just never went back that day.

The apartment was full of men Kiana knew. I slept on the sofa in the living room, and as I rolled over to get more comfortable and opened my eyes, I saw one of the men sitting next to me in a chair. He was just staring at me in the darkness, not saying a word. My heart sank, and my nerves were shot when I finally had the courage to ask him what he was doing. "Looking at you," he said in a slow, quiet voice. I had a bad feeling about this, so I got up fast and told him to go away. I was not going to let him touch me.

I grabbed my backpack and took off. I did not sleep for the rest of the night. It felt like days of waiting outside for the sun to come up. I walked to my school and waited for the janitor to open the door at six o'clock in the morning to clean. I told him I was there to do makeup work and meet the teacher when he asked me why I had shown up so early.

I went to the bathroom and washed my hair in the sink, using the hand soap the school provided—my hair was so dried out it looked horrible. Not having conditioner sucked. Tying it back was the only way to look half-decent. I slept as much as I could in class because I was so tired. Five minutes felt like thirty to me, but every minute of sleep was precious to me and well worth it.

Somehow my mother found out about that incident and talked to my friend's mom. I'm not sure what was said exactly, but after that, I lived with Kiki and her mom for a while. Following her mom's rules was easy, and I was so happy to do so. We ate dinner together as a family, we watched TV together, and I went to bed at a regular hour. Sleep was still hard for me because I was so used to sleeping with "one eye open," meaning I had to always be alert mentally and be prepared if something were to happen.

The best part of all was that there was no yelling and fighting, no beatings and blaming me for every single problem that arose. I felt like I was in heaven. For the first time, I could relax my whole body and soul, and I didn't want it to end.

I was learning things in school now, thinking about who I was inside, what I wanted to be in life, what I wanted to do, and when I attended college. One day, my friend's mom told me that my mother had moved two hours away. She never said goodbye or told me where she was going.

I was more thankful that I didn't have to be concerned about what my mother was going to do next. I had no real worries at all. I just dreamt about the things I wanted in life: a family of my own, with kids to love and cherish the way my parents never did for me.

I wasn't into destroying my body with all the things the people around me were doing. All they wanted to do was smoke weed and drink, have casual sex, and who knows what else. Sex, to me, was not what the others thought it was. I was hurt so badly the first time that I hated sex and did not want to be the girl who just had sex for her own enjoyment. I think the real reason was that I was afraid of sex, drugs, and alcohol because I did not want to get hurt. I wanted to be there 100 percent mentally so bad things wouldn't happen to me.

Things seemed to be going smoothly for once until I came home one day to my friend hanging out with my ex-boyfriend—he had no idea I lived there. Shortly after that, he became her boyfriend, and I was absolutely disgusted with him. Why my friend? And why was I staying in that apartment when he was there making out with her? I ended up leaving every time he came over and made different friends because she was too involved with him. I was slowly starting to find my way out of the situation.

It didn't happen fast enough though. One day, I was sitting on a bench at the park, waiting for a friend to pick me up so we could go to the movies. Kiana confronted me with her boyfriend and said, "I heard you were talking shit about us." I told her I wasn't, but she continued to instigate a fight and pushed me to the ground. When I got up, we were surrounded by a group of people. Every time I tried to leave, they kept pushing me back toward her.

"Why are you doing this? He just wants to see us fight," I pleaded.

She insisted that her boyfriend had said he heard me and told her all about it. I looked down and saw that she had pulled out a knife, and I went into this weird trance. I looked around for something to protect myself with while I stayed conscious of my hair and shirt, knowing that if she grabbed either one, she would be able to stab me. We were in a grassy area, but there were no rocks, sticks, or hard objects to throw at her.

Kiana kept getting closer, and I was running out of time. I started to think of ways to get away. My adrenaline was out of control, but I finally noticed a burned-out barbeque grill by the table I had been sitting on before she came. It was all I had. As she came at me, I instinctively grabbed a handful of charcoal and threw it at her. She started screaming, and that's when I realized it had been hot. She grabbed her face, and everyone gathered around her. I felt bad. I didn't mean to hurt her, so I just ran away.

My friend saw me walking and picked me up in his Honda, wondering if I was ready to see the movie. He took me to a movie and then to dinner. We talked about the fight that night, and he told me to just keep moving forward, not to sweat the small stuff. I was so mad at him though. He thought I was just some out-of-control teenager going from house to house. He had no idea what I was going through.

When I returned to the apartment, her mother slapped me. She was so mad at me. She was asking me how I could do that to her daughter after everything they had done for me. I kept telling her I was sorry, and I tried to tell her that Kiana had pulled a knife on me, but she would not listen to anything I had to say. My friend didn't say a word to me when she came out of her room, and I apologized, but she had a patch on her left eye.

There was a knock at the door; it was the police. They walked inside and asked who Jessica was, and I was terrified when I had to tell them that it was me. They wanted to know where my mother was, but I honestly did not know and told them that she just left me with these people when she took off. My friend's mom went on to tell them that my mother had said she wasn't able to handle me anymore and that she had agreed to watch over me until I had now become too much for her. The officer had no idea what my life had been like or what had really happened earlier that day, and I was too afraid to speak up. I just let him assume whatever he wanted to about me. He told me to pack my things because I was going to the police station.

As I sat in the police car, I felt so tired of never being able to get anywhere in life. Things were going just fine until my ex stepped back into the picture. I was back to not knowing what would happen next. I felt so alone and confused. Why was I so cursed to live this kind of life? When we got to the police department, they let me make one phone call.

I called my friend who had taken me out earlier that night and thanked him for his friendship, knowing that was probably the last time I would ever see him. He was mad that nothing happened to the other girl and that I was being punished for defending myself. I was in juvenile hall for a week.

During my time there, I was treated well. I slept in my own room, ate three meals a day, and had a very comfortable bed. The food was pretty good too. One morning while I was making my bed, the officers told me that my mother was coming to pick me up and that I should get my things ready to go. I felt so sick. I didn't want her to pick me up from this place. At the same time, I wondered how Vanessa was; I couldn't wait to see her face! I waited for her in the lobby, where parents visited their kids. As I was sitting there, I thought of all the beatings, the way my mother's eyes looked, and the smell of her spit dripping down my face when she was finished beating me up. I was so scared to see her face again.

She talked with one of the male officers in his office for a while before she took me home. I wondered what they were talking about, what type of drama was spilling from my mother's mouth. I prayed that he was grilling her with questions on where she had been all this time, why she had left me with strangers, and why I was so shy and wouldn't speak to the staff members the whole time I was here. I wanted her to get in trouble for all the things she had done to me.

But no, a half hour later, she came out giggling and walking behind him. Again, I was not surprised that she got away with what she had been doing. She always laughed that certain laugh when she got what she wanted or was trying to get what she wanted from a man. I was free to go, but he did say one last thing to me while we were walking to the car though: "Be good for your mom, and don't let me catch you in here again." I regretted not telling him everything. I just didn't think he would believe me—my feelings at the time were so complicated.

The ride home was mostly spent in silence, and I was afraid of what she had planned for me because my sister was not with her. I wanted so badly to ask her where Vanessa was, but I had learned long ago not to start conversations with my mother, and this wouldn't be a good time to begin. I just sat there, staring out the window, looking at the road. It was too quiet in the car.

She finally broke the silence and asked me something, "Why couldn't you just stay away?" She went on to tell me what a great life she and my sister had now and that I was going to mess everything up again. I told her that I would stay out of her way, but she mocked me in a snotty, sarcastic voice, repeating what I had just said. She told me that she had moved to Foster City, California, and they were living in an apartment by the beach.

When we got there, it was so nice, and I was so excited to see my sister, but I sort of pushed her away when she hugged me because I did not want our mother to see her happiness. Mother always hated to see us happy together, and I had just gotten home and didn't want to make her mad.

My mom worked a lot with her clients, and my sister and I went to parks and hung out at the beach while she worked in the house. One day, her boyfriend she dated for a long time came to see my mom. He told her that he had not seen me in so long, and he remembered when I was little. He told her I was growing older and looking good. My mom was mad and told me to get in the house.

She came in when he left, and there she went, telling me I should have stayed away, and now her boyfriend liked me. I do not think he meant it the way she took it. My sister came into the living room and told my mom to please stop and not do this again. My mom kept talking about it, and my sister fell to the floor, screaming at me that I should have stayed away. She told me that their life was so much better when I was gone.

My mom said, "See? Even your sister admits it is better when you're gone." I wanted to get out of that house so badly. My brother came back with us after finding out where we lived from some relatives, and I was happy to see him. He told me all his stories while he was away, and I told him mine.

Chapter 8

Escort Life of a Teen

We moved by a lake in Oakland, California. Our mother was working from home again, so we had to be gone most of the day. We ate at different places around town and hung out on the lake, saving animals. One day, there was an oil spill, and we saw turtles trying to escape. I knew I had to do something, so I jumped into the lake, grabbed as many turtles as I could find, and gave them to Vanessa, who put them in a big bag.

We brought the turtles home and put them in a children's plastic pool in the backyard. Vanessa told our mother about what happened, and since she was an animal lover, she helped by taking us to a big lake that was much better than where they were, with clean water. I felt amazing that day because I saved turtles.

Our mother ended up having to partner with another lady in the escort business. I was surprised she had a coworker of any kind because my mother was a very jealous person and never had any friends, as she viewed females as a threat. Their relationship got out of hand after working together for a while. That lady was bossy and made my mom drive her to all her appointments. She also took most of the clients, leaving my mother to take her frustrations out on me. I did my best to stay out of the way, but my mother did not have control of her own business anymore, so she was always upset and looking for me to beat on.

I remember going to that lady's house one day. There were young girls, from about fifteen years old and up, giving massages and sex for money. There was one girl my age, only fourteen years old, the niece of my mother's partner. The girl told me it was her first time working there that day because she wanted a new pair of shoes. I told her she didn't have to do that as she was getting dressed in her sexy work outfit—she was young but had curves and an adult body.

We watched a man come in, talk to her aunt, and then give her money before he went into one of the rooms. The girl whispered to her aunt, "It's only sex, right?" and her aunt said, "Yes, don't worry. It will go fast, and then you can go get your shoes." I wanted to stop her from walking in there, but I knew I had no right to even try. I watched the door slowly close, and my heart hurt knowing what was about to happen in that room, knowing she would regret what was about to happen for the rest of her life.

I sat there on the sofa in the living room, listening and thinking about what I should do when I heard her cry. As she screamed, I got up and tried to open the door, but it was locked. I started banging and yelling for him to stop. Her aunt grabbed me and told me to go outside. As she dragged me to the front door, all I heard was her yelling, "It hurts! Stop it!" I didn't want to leave, but I had to.

I stood outside the door for another forty-five minutes until he left, and they let me back in the house. The girl was crying on the bed and yelling at her aunt because he had stuck his dick in her butt—she didn't know he was going to do that. Her aunt told her that was just part of sex and gave her seventy-five dollars for the work but kept the rest.

The girl said to her aunt, "This is not enough for my shoes."

Her aunt said, "Well, it looks like we need to make you another appointment to make more money."

The look on the girl's face was so sad as if she was going to go for it.

I knew her aunt had pocketed more money for pimping out her own niece than what she gave the girl for having to endure anal raping. That poor girl could hardly walk to the next room. I was numb as to what I had just witnessed. I felt so bad for her and angry with myself because I couldn't help her. I wasn't allowed to be around their clients anymore after that.

In the next few weeks, my mother slowly shifted away from that lady and started to work on her own again. Living in a world with no father figure and seeing different men in and out of the house paying for sex with girls thirteen and up as a child was hard because I felt that all men were assholes who could never be trusted.

My mother was going with her usual, telling me how much she hated me and how horrible her life was. I lay in my bed, pretending to be asleep, waiting for what she was going to do next, listening to her pace back and forth. I kept falling asleep and waking up in fear, seemingly minutes later, listening to my mother. When I thought she had gone to bed, I closed my eyes and fell asleep.

I woke up to her grabbing me by my hair, dragging me to the bathroom, and slapping me in the face. I was so tired, and all I wanted to do was go to bed. This time, my mother grabbed an electric hair shaver from under the sink and then plugged it into the wall. I was sitting on the toilet in tears. "Oh, poor thing, you don't want your haircut?" she mocked. I shook my head no, hoping she wasn't going to do it, but she grabbed a big chunk of my hair and started to cut it three inches away from my scalp.

I cried more than ever that night as she took her time destroying my hair. I had never wanted to die as much as I did that night. I was always able to hide how she made me feel inside, but that night I cried and screamed like I never had in my life. I felt my image and soul being destroyed. As if it was not bad enough, she made me wear the same dirty clothes to school. Now everyone was going to make fun of me because of my messed-up hair.

When she was finally done, she had this sick look on her face, so happy that she was able to hurt me like never before. The rush she got from watching me cry my eyes out was disgusting. I never cried when she beat me or yelled at me the way I did when she gave me this horribly uneven, crooked boy's haircut. She was so pleased with herself because she broke me that night.

She even made me grab a broom and clean up the hair on the floor afterward. I took a shower and, for a minute, forgot about what she had done to my hair. When I went to shampoo my hair, I felt how short it was and began to cry quietly, afraid of her hearing me. I washed what was left of my hair and felt so weak from holding the pain in. It was hard to breathe. I wished I could scream and let it all out. I didn't have the guts to look in the mirror after I got out of the shower, so I just grabbed my towel, dressed, and went to bed.

Morning arrived, and I got dressed, almost forgetting about my hair. I went to brush my teeth in the bathroom, where the horrible event had taken place the night before. Slowly, I glanced in the mirror, and all I felt was a pain in my chest. I looked like a crazy crackhead! It was beyond bad and uneven! I didn't know how I was going to make it through school like that. My mother came to my room and told me I couldn't wear a hooded sweatshirt to school because she wanted everyone to see my new haircut.

As I walked to school, I came across a box sitting outside for the Salvation Army to pick up, and inside was a black boys' dress hat, so I put it on, and it fit. I had no idea how I looked in it, and I didn't care either—anything to cover what was left of my hair! When I arrived at school, I headed straight to the bathroom to look in the mirror, and I did not look so bad with the hat.

I had some makeup and put on a little eyeliner, some mascara, and lipstick. I thought I looked stylish and hoped none of the teachers would tell me to take my hat off in class. Thankfully, I made it through the whole day without anyone saying a thing.

When school was over, I slipped into the bathroom and washed my face but kept my hat on for the walk home. About a block away, I took it off and hid it in my backpack, all the way at the bottom, and I even messed up my hair so my mother would think I had walked around like that all day.

When I came home, she was getting ready for work, so I went to my room, thinking she had forgotten about my hair. She came to my room and said she hoped my day was horrible and told me to watch my sister while she worked that night.

DIABOLICAL IN DISGUISE

From then on, I wore that hat every day until my hair grew out. People asked me why I never took it off, but I never answered them. I was too scared to talk to anyone. I'm pretty sure everyone thought I was a freak. Once my hair grew out, I tossed that hat in the garbage, hoping that would never happen again.

I started going to ROTC because I had a plan to go into the Army after high school. If I was going to die, I wanted it to be for a good cause, and if I didn't die, I wanted to be able to go to college. I tried to think of ways I could get away from my mother sooner, but all I could do was count the years until I turned eighteen.

I was cooking for my mother and Vanessa one night as they watched my mom's favorite show, *The X-Files*. The night was good so far. My mom had her glass of wine, and I was cooking spaghetti. I wanted to get everything out on the plate hot and tried to cook everything at the same time, forgetting that the breaker in the kitchen would blow if I used too many electrical devices. My mother was so angry when it happened. She told me how stupid I was because of how many times she had already told me that would happen. My mother didn't care that I was trying to get all her food out on time so she'd have a hot meal.

After our mother went outside to flip the breaker, Vanessa and I knew she wasn't going to let this one go. I was prepared for whatever happened next, or so I thought. "Why are you so stupid? Why are you still alive? Why don't you just kill yourself?" she said as she came back inside the house. She grabbed a frying pan and started to chase me around the kitchen and hit me on my head before I could duck to protect myself. I covered my head with both hands as she kept hitting me over and over again.

My hands were burning with each hit, but at least I was protecting my head. She broke my left pinkie with one of her last strikes. After she dropped the frying pan, she grabbed a knife, and I jumped to my feet and yelled out, "Why don't I just leave right now? I'll leave for good!"

I immediately went into my room and packed my things at 10:00 p.m. Outside, it was cold, and as I walked to the lake across the street, I thought to myself, *Here we go again*. I hated being alone and in the dark outside. I was so tired I found a bench to sit on near a park light. My adrenaline was pumping so hard that my body was anything but relaxed. As I sat there, looking at the streetlights reflecting off the lake, I could not believe how many people were exercising this late at night.

My pinkie hurt so badly; I could not believe she had broken it. I sat there by myself, trying to think about how I would go about fixing my finger myself. I sat there for the longest time, trying to think of what to do next when my mother drove up and saw me sitting on the bench. She pulled over and told me to get in the car. I wanted to tell her no, but I knew I couldn't. I was cold and tired, so I stood and went with her.

She told me there had to be a legal way to get me out of the house so the police wouldn't keep bringing me back home. She couldn't handle the stress of how much she hated me anymore, and I needed to leave her house so she could be happy.

At school the next day, I sought information on emancipation. I found out that if I had good grades, a job that paid the rent at my own place, and good school attendance on my own, I could be free from my mother. I told her, and she liked the idea, but I needed to hurry because she wanted me out.

By then, Pete had his own apartment with a bunch of his friends. I asked him if I could stay there until I got a job and was able to be emancipated, but he didn't think it was a good idea at first. I had to beg him and tell him what our mother had been doing to me, and I made him feel guilty for leaving. He finally broke down and let me stay on the sofa, his only rule being that I stay away from his friends. That was an easy rule to follow because I didn't want to be around them anyway! They hardly ever slept and did not even pay rent for staying there—they were a bunch of freeloaders.

Everyone there partied hard. While I was trying to get some sleep for school the next day, one of my brother's friends was jumping on the other couch and playing his electric guitar loudly while my brother and his friends were all having a great time. When I told them to quit because I had school in the morning, the guitarist jumped off the couch, and they all ran to a window.

They were talking about jumping out and flying like Superman, but we were on the twenty-fifth floor of the building! I told them to stop getting so close to the window because they were freaking me out, but none of them cared. They kept telling Pete to fly out the window, pushing his head out the window, and cheering him on to jump.

I yelled at Pete to please come back inside, or he was going to die if he jumped, but it was useless to keep yelling at them. I was afraid that if I kept at them, they would try to prove a point—that they could really fly like Superman. I did my best to stay calm and block out what they were doing, and I eventually fell asleep.

I didn't want to be awake if they did something stupid, and I didn't want to wake up to see the aftermath of their stupidity. When I woke up at 5:00 a.m., they were asleep, scattered all over the floor, with my brother near the door. I went to school that day and never stayed at his place ever again.

CHAPTER 9

Married at Fifteen

I ASKED MY MOTHER IF I COULD stay at her place again until I found a job and was emancipated, but she told me she had found another legal way to get rid of me for good. She asked about that man I met once and asked me if he liked me. I told her I talked to him but was not sure if he liked me.

My mom had him as a client and noticed his interest in me. She said he was one who needed a US citizen to marry him to "fix his papers" and make him a legal US citizen. I'd have to live with him so it looked real, but it was going to be better than staying with my mother—I knew it. *Who could be worse than her?* I thought.

We both met with him the next day. His name was Ramon, and he was a dark-skinned Latino and incredibly quiet. His English was so bad that, at times, my mother and I had trouble understanding what he was saying. I didn't know his ethnicity or what country he was from. All I knew at the time was that this Spanish-speaking guy could be my ticket out of hell.

My mother talked with him about how the deal was going to be done. After our marriage was arranged, I had the opportunity to ask him where he was from, and he told me, "Costa Rica." At fifteen, I had no idea where that was or what race that would make him. I didn't understand what "fixing papers" really meant either. He made it sound so easy, just fake our marriage for a little bit, sign some things, and fix his papers. Then I would be able to get away from my mother and create my own life. It seemed like a win-win situation.

As a thank-you, my mother paid him for "getting rid of her problem." Later that week, she took me to the Salvation Army, where I found a cute wedding dress in my size for only twelve dollars. I can't really describe how I felt during this time in my life. Part of me was excited to start a new life, and the other part of me was terrified of the unknown. I was about to marry a grown man at fifteen years old. For the second time in my life, my mother had sold me off for her own benefit.

Within a month, we were on our way to a chapel in Reno, Nevada, to get married. Everything happened so fast. My mother told me she was excited that I was finally growing up, no longer her responsibility.

I sat there feeling angry with my mother, so angry that she had just signed me off to some stranger. I was sort of relieved to finally get out of her house but afraid of what would happen once this was finalized, when I would become his property. I looked at the man I was about to marry and wondered if he was nice. He seemed nice, but what was he really like?

I sat there dreaming about getting this over with, winning my freedom, finishing school, and joining the Army. I had so many mixed emotions. I was nervous, scared, and happy all at the same time. More than anything, I just wanted to be away from my mother, but was it the right decision? It really didn't matter what my worries were though. I had no other options.

Finally, it was our turn to be married, and my mother sat with a smile as our witness. The priest told us to step up and asked if we had gone to counseling before we decided to get married. I told him we had not, but then Ramon interrupted me, telling the man that while he knew I was young, he truly did love me and that my mother approved. I agreed, hoping for it to work so I wouldn't have to go back home with my mother. Who knows what she would have done if she found out this plan of hers did not work?

We succeeded in making the man believe we were happy and in love, and we were married. I gave my new husband a peck on the lips, our first kiss together. We then took pictures for the immigration department to help convince them that this was a real marriage.

I felt so sick and couldn't believe my life had changed so drastically with just one signature. It was as if I had sold my soul to the devil, and my mother was pleased about it. I was a child, and I didn't even know how I was going to become a wife to this man and how I was going to get out so I could be free from everyone. I knew I did not want to have sex with him at all, but at the end of the day, I also knew it might not be my choice to make.

The fake wedding was over, and we drove back to California. As I looked out the window, I felt emotionally exhausted and did not know what was coming next. I ended up splitting ways from my mom and going to Ramon's apartment. He rented a room from these people from El Salvador. They seemed nice. I thought I could leave if I wanted to, but I was too scared.

I didn't want to run the risk of upsetting him in any way. The next night, he left and was gone all night. He didn't come back until around five the next morning. After a while, he finally told me he had been working at Denny's restaurant. My gullible young mind thought we would live together for a little bit like roommates to make this look legitimate before he went his way and I went mine.

When he introduced me to his friends and family, the first thing out of all their mouths was "Are you going to fix his papers?" I was just a key to fixing their issue and not a person. I was nothing to them. It made me feel used, unloved, and alone on a whole new level. I was beginning to regret what I had chosen, having to deal with these strangers on my own, but it was still better than living with my mother.

I wanted to go back and finish school, but Ramon told me to look for a job. I knew I needed to have money to support myself, so I started working the graveyard shift at a Kwik Way hamburger place in Oakland, California. He made sure I went to work too, telling my boss to give me more hours and informing him how much he thought I should be paid. My boss obviously didn't like him and often asked me why I was with him because I was so young. I had nothing to say except for the fact that I needed this job, and I didn't want anything to get in the way of that. I continued to work long hours and loved it because it was better than sitting around the apartment with nothing to do.

When I got off work, Ramon would be parked in the car outside, waiting to drive me home. I thought he cared about my safety when he did this and wanted to make sure I had a ride home. This lasted for a few weeks until I got off one night, and he wasn't there. I waited, and it was going on 2:30 a.m., but he never showed up.

I remembered that one of his friends lived a few blocks away, so I began walking the streets in the dark to see if he was there. I was lost for a moment but finally found the house that looked like where his friends lived, and I peeked through the window of the living room. He was sitting there with all his friends, having a great time. They were sitting on the sofa with a coffee table full of cocaine, and one of the guys was taking his turn, snorting it up.

I knocked on the door and asked him what he was doing. He told his friends in Spanish that he had to leave. I walked toward his car and waited for him to unlock it when he asked me if I saw anything. I told him yes and that he disgusted me. That was a big mistake.

He slammed me against the side of the car, slapped me in the face, grabbed me by my neck, and said, "Don't you ever talk to me like that. I do whatever I want, and you were supposed to wait for me at work." This was the first time he ever laid a hand on me, and I almost pissed my pants at that moment.

On the ride home, I felt sick to my stomach, thinking about how stupid I was to marry this foreign man I didn't even know. What was I being punished for? I must have done something to deserve all that was happening to me.

I walked up the wooden stairs in the back of the house to his apartment. He opened the door, and I went to the bathroom to cry. I felt trapped and had no one to call or talk to about what had just happened. I kept telling myself to just forget about it and go to sleep, but when I came out, he told me to get on his bed, not the sofa.

My body became numb all over as he yelled at me again and ordered me to get on his bed. I sat down, and he started to kiss me. All I wanted to do was run away, but I knew it would only get worse. I just gave in—I gave in like I had with my stepfather, my first boyfriend, and my mother. I knew time would pass by like a dream, as it had always done before, and things would move along less painfully if I did what he asked.

He took my clothes off, piece by piece, but when he had me down to my underwear, I froze. I kept my hands over my private parts and stiffened up. Instead of feeling bad for scaring me, he got forceful and made me take off my bra and underwear. I did what he told me to do and just kept my eyes closed and thought of some sort of fantasy to take me away. I sang a song in my head like I used to do when my mother was beating me.

I did not realize that I had blacked out to the point where I had no idea I was having sex with him. I opened my eyes to his frustration.

"What? You can't feel me?" I didn't say a word. He disgusted me, and I didn't want to feel him. I wanted him to leave me alone. He kept asking me why I wasn't moaning, that I must like big dicks, and he must be too small.

My silence only made him more aggressive. I yelled for someone to help me, but he covered my mouth with his hand, his eyes wild from the cocaine he had snorted earlier. He started shoving his hand in my vagina. I could feel it burning as it tore. "You like that? Is that big enough for you?" he yelled at me. I was so terrified I couldn't scream, let alone move. I just lay there wondering why I couldn't get away from this hell. Why the hell was I even there? When he was finally done, he passed out naked, and I went to the bathroom to cry my eyes out. I lay there on the floor, crying as quietly as I could so he wouldn't wake up and hurt me again. I rocked myself to sleep, pretending I was rocking my soul, telling myself it was okay to sleep like a baby trying to soothe myself to sleep.

Morning came, and he woke up happy and refreshed. "Good morning!" he said to me, accompanied with a smile. I felt so dirty and ashamed of myself, not knowing what to expect from this rapist—this rapist I happened to be married to, whom I belonged to.

He told me to lie next to him, and I did. He asked me why I looked so sad. I told him how much pain I was in and that he'd hurt me, but he looked at me in disbelief. He yelled at me again, denying what he had done, and told me it was all inside my head and none of what I said was true. Then he began to make up reasons for why he did it, saying it was my fault and I had done it to myself, and then he acted like nothing had happened.

I remember that terrified feeling I had when I was with my mother. It was like how I felt when I learned my mom had plotted to kill my aunt, and reality sank in, knowing just how dangerous she was. He had done something to me with such anger and did not remember it. Every moment was like a ticking time bomb after this.

Time flew by rather quickly. Minutes became hours, and days became months. I had to go with him to different events and get-togethers with his friends, pretending I was happy. I pretended I was an actress, playing a successful, happy wife. I blocked all my emotions and sucked up my feelings so he would look good and be happy.

After a few months, Ramon gradually became more abusive. He called me stupid every day and garbage because I could not do anything right in his eyes. This was nothing new for me because my mom had said far worse things to me growing up.

Chapter 10

A Child Who Changed My Life

HE CONTINUED TO HAVE SEX WITH ME after that, never caring that I didn't want it. I was his piece of property, filling more than just the need to fix his papers. Having sex with a mean man made me feel so dirty, and I felt so disgusted with myself. I knew if I pretended to enjoy it, he wouldn't hurt me like he did otherwise.

I was working a shift at Kwik Way when I suddenly felt dizzy and ran to the bathroom to throw up. I remember the horrible smell of the greasy restaurant that day, but I pulled myself together and worked all day even though I was feeling sick. The motions of the bus ride home didn't help. As soon as I got off, I fell to the ground, and a lady helped me to a bus stop bench.

She asked if I was okay. I had thought that maybe it was just the flu. When I started to walk the five blocks home, I threw up every other half block.

It was another lonely part of my life because I had no one to talk to. I was scared because I was only sixteen years old and did not have insurance or enough money to go to a doctor. Finally, I made it home and went to my room to lie down, thinking I would feel better when I woke up. I felt worse the next morning.

Ramon came home shortly after I woke up, and I told him I didn't feel well and that I needed the day off. I spent two days at home after that, feeling horrible. He finally found a cheap clinic that I could go to. When we were there, the doctor noticed our big age difference and asked if we were married.

She wanted to talk to me alone and asked about my relationship with Ramon after he left. I shut down because I didn't like people asking me questions about my life. I was scared to answer truthfully. What if I told her everything and he found out? Everything would be worse then—he would just hurt me even worse. She finally asked me whether I would keep the baby if I was pregnant. I said that I would and asked her what this had to do with me having the flu. She told me that my test results came back positive, so I was pregnant. I was in shock and had no idea what to say.

I had no clue as to how I was going to protect a child. I couldn't even take care of myself. I sat there soaking it in, waiting for the doctor to get Ramon from the waiting area to tell him the news, thinking of how there was a fetus growing inside me—I was pregnant.

I thought about how I had always wanted a family to protect and take care of, so I began to get excited. Then Ramon walked through the door, and that feeling of excitement quickly turned into worry. He walked into the room, and I told him I was pregnant, but he instantly smiled, so that meant he was okay with it.

From there, we applied for medical aid, and he took me for a big strawberry milkshake. He started taking really good care of me after that like a real husband would. He never hit me during my pregnancy, and I began to think he would change for the better. I thought maybe I would have a good influence on him and learn to love him. I started to eat more and have more energy as my pregnancy went on. I ate all sorts of weird things, like strawberry ice cream over garlic bread, mangos, and beef-tongue tacos.

My baby was always moving around when I went for checkups, so we did not know its sex. I hoped I was having a girl so I could dress her up all the time. I'd protect her from evil and dream about all the good things I would be able to do for her—the things no one ever did for me.

We moved close to Ramon's work, near Benicia, California, and rented a room from a good friend of Ramon's, and they accepted that I was pregnant. It was a nice house, and I had my own space. Ramon worked long shifts that allowed me to sleep basically all day and eat a lot. I rested more than I ever had. I was comfortable in their home.

I went to the school district to see if I could do home study and earn my diploma. I had to get my transcripts from my other school, so I asked Ramon to take me to my old school in Oakland. He said that I did not need to go back to school and that I needed to find a job to support us as soon as the baby was born. I was so sad because I wanted to finish school.

I also wanted to have my baby on my birthday, February 22, so I walked up and down hills and rode a bike. I tried so hard but ended up not being able to have it on my birthday.

One day during the last term of my pregnancy, I went to the petting zoo. I was feeding the goats and sheep when a ram started to stare me down. He had a mean look on his face and then began to breathe heavily. He charged at me and rammed me to the ground. I was not at all prepared for that, and it felt like a car had run me over! I stood up as fast as I could and left the park. I didn't feel anything at first because I was in shock, but then I suddenly started to feel labor pains. The pains started happening closer together, and sure enough, I was on my way to the hospital to have my first child.

I was dilated five centimeters when I first arrived at the hospital. The birth wasn't easy. I threw up the entire time, and at one point, there were four male doctors pressing on my stomach as I pushed. They had to cut me so the baby would fit through the birth canal. Ramon passed out from the sight of all the blood.

I pushed so hard that I felt a hot burning sensation and a big pop. The doctor yelled out, "It's a boy!" I could not see my baby at first because my eyes were watering so much, but as I blinked, I began to see clearly and saw the doctor holding my baby boy. I could not believe I'd just had a baby boy on February 27, 1997. He was the most beautiful boy I had ever seen. I heard him cry, a more unique cry than any other baby, and he weighed nine pounds ten ounces and was twenty-two inches long. His head was bald, perfectly round, and he had ivory-white skin. He had the cutest newborn baby smell. When he cried, I held his little hand, and he stopped crying. And as I let go, he cried, so I would hold his hand again, and he would stop crying. I believe I made him feel safe, and I knew then I was meant to protect him.

When Ramon entered the room and held our son, the first thing he did was ask if the baby was his. I was shocked, wondering how he could ask such a thing. He started talking to me aggressively as I lay there in the hospital bed just moments after I had finally given birth to our child. He held our son and told me the baby was too white to be his.

I feared what he was going to do next and wanted him to give me my baby back. I knew we were in a public place, but I also knew there was no stopping him when he was mad. I quietly tried to explain to him that my genes were strong because of my grandfather's side of the family, genetics that was strongly present in all my family. I was so happy when Ramon finally sat down and said how cute the baby was. He left the hospital shortly after that while I stayed the night.

The nurses asked what his name would be, and I had never once thought of a name for him because I thought he was going to be a girl. I knew I wanted to continue my grandpa's middle name, so I picked Joseph. Ramon wanted to name him Jake, so Jake Joseph it was. I had never been in love as much as I loved Jake.

That night was the most beautiful night I had ever had in my life. I got to hold my baby until the next day. It was like a dream come true. I now had a son, and I got to name him Jake. I woke to hear him crying later that night, and I knew he was hungry. I wanted the best for him and wanted to breastfeed as much as possible, but I had no idea how.

I was so thankful when the nurse came in and showed me how. He latched on like a little pro, and I caught on quickly. I was young and felt alone in the world, but I now had this little boy named Jake in my arms, and it was my son and me. I knew I had to do whatever it took to protect my baby. I did not want what happened to me, my brother, and my sister to happen to my boy. I wanted the best for him and had this love like no other. My life became more meaningful one day because I had something to call my own, and I had a sense of purpose.

Chapter 11

Having a Child Never Changed His Ways

After I brought Jake home from the hospital, I went back to living in fear of my husband daily. I had such a hard time sleeping. After about three months of staying home with Jake, Ramon told me I had to get a job, so I applied at Denny's restaurant. Ramon sat by my side through the interview and talked for me, asking what hours they had and how many I could work a day. The manager was confused and asked why he was talking for me.

Ramon was a very charming guy who usually got his way, so he told the manager that he wanted to make sure I landed the job because we just had a baby and needed to work. I was so afraid the manager would tell him I was unable to work there because of my controlling husband. Sure enough, I was hired, and I was so shocked and relieved because now it would be one less thing for him to be angry about.

I worked twelve-hour shifts, and Ramon brought Jake twice a day so I could breastfeed him. My breasts became infected from long hours without breastfeeding. They were in pain and leaking all the time. After a few months of working, we moved into our own apartment. It was very nice, with a pool, a gym, a laundry room, a kids' park, and a hangout lounge. I was skinny and looked tired all the time because I worked the graveyard shift and then took care of my baby during the day. I was hooked on Red Bull because it helped me focus and stay awake.

Jake was growing up so fast, and he was the cutest kid! He started to walk at ten months old, and we walked around outside a lot. It was nice spending time with him alone while Ramon was at work. I felt at peace, teaching him what I knew was good for him and focusing on Jake instead of whatever Ramon might do next.

Ramon had taken away my independence. I literally had to ask him for everything and had no say in our marriage at all. He constantly broke me down and told me how stupid I was. If I made the littlest mistake, he would go on and on about how stupid I was for hours.

His abuse grew progressively worse, and I'd go to work with black eyes from him hitting me for the smallest things, like if his food was not the way he had wanted it. I felt so stuck, and I thought that if I left, he would take my baby away from me. There was no one I could turn to for help.

I carried on, day in and day out, and worked to pay our rent and to pay off the fines, tickets, and court fees Ramon had accumulated. As soon as his record was cleaned up enough, we went to the immigration office to file the application for his citizenship papers. Twice a month, we had to stand in line for five hours and then sit down for three more hours to speak with the immigration directors.

One time, he was angry when we left because things weren't going the way he wanted them to. Jake was sleeping so peacefully in the back seat of the car, but Ramon didn't care and started to yell at me. He told me I was useless and I was garbage to him because I was unable to get his green card.

I asked him if he believed in God, and he just became angrier and told me that if there were a god, then he would have his papers by now. "God only helps people who deserve the blessing," I said to him. He grabbed me by my hair and repeatedly slammed my head against the window. Then he pulled over to the side of the freeway.

He started punching me in the stomach and telling me that he should just dump me off on the side of the road. I begged him not to and took responsibility for talking to him like that, saying I never should have. I told him I would be the perfect wife and always do whatever he wanted from then on.

My begging worked, and we drove away in awkward silence. I sat there listening to the radio, just happy that my baby was safe and that I was allowed to come home. I learned how to calm him down and just tell him what he wanted to hear after that.

No one knew what I was going through. I didn't trust anyone to help me. In my mind, I was thinking that if I told others the truth about Ramon, they would take away my baby and send me back to live with my mother. So I went home with him and did what I thought would help me stay with and protect my baby.

We moved to another city to be closer to Ramon's job shortly after that. I tried to get back into school, but he told me I needed to work. He controlled my every move, just like when I went for my interview at the restaurant.

He made sure I worked more than eight hours a day, and he even watched me from the parking lot when he wasn't working. I don't know how he had so much influence on my new boss, but he had me working fifteen hours a day, knowing I was only sixteen years old.

I began to feel sick at work again, so the first thing I did was take a pregnancy test: negative. I went to take a nap with Jake, but when I woke up to use the bathroom, I had the urge to check the test one more time. I couldn't believe it: positive. I took another test in the morning, and I was indeed pregnant and had no idea how to tell Ramon. I was going to be too sick to work and bring money in, so I didn't know how well he would take the news.

When I told him, he was shocked but said that if I was on welfare, it wouldn't bother him if I didn't work, and for that, I was thankful. I did what I had to do to keep peace in the house with Ramon. It was hard to keep up with Jake during my second pregnancy, but I managed. Cooking was the hardest thing to do because of the smell.

I had gone to the doctor for a checkup and blood work. Things seemed okay with my growing baby, and I was so happy. I wondered if I was having a boy or a girl, but if it was a healthy baby, I would be grateful.

I was around four months pregnant, and I went in for my second ultrasound. They said I was having a girl but had seen something that caused concern for my baby girl. The doctors told Ramon and me that our baby could possibly have Down syndrome. They saw through the ultrasound that the back of her neck had a lump that could indicate this.

They said since Ramon was thirteen years older than me led them to think there was more of a chance. The doctor asked me whether I wanted to abort my baby if she, in fact, had Down syndrome. Ramon did not think twice and yelled out, "Yes!"

I immediately said, "No!"

The doctor said to go home to talk it over, but we had to decide soon.

Ramon never gave me an opportunity to discuss it and said if the test showed that she had Down syndrome, then we were going to abort her. I grabbed my belly and closed my eyes. I prayed that the test confirmed she did not have it. I was happy she was inside me because I could protect her from him.

One night when I was six months pregnant, I was feeding Jake in his high chair and was happy because I'd made Ramon's dinner to his satisfaction for once. Our son was fussy and not wanting to eat anymore, but when I moved to take him out of his chair, Ramon grabbed me and pushed me to the side, yelling, "He is going to eat all his food!" I told him that Jake wasn't hungry anymore and just needed to sleep. I was doing my best to stay calm, but I was scared for my child.

Ramon took the spoon and started shoving food into Jake's mouth. When he started crying and shaking his head no, I went into a rage. I pushed Ramon away, took Jake out of the high chair, and tried to run outside, but Ramon grabbed me by my hair and pulled me to the ground. I didn't let go of Jake until Ramon started to punch me in the face.

Jake was screaming and crying, and Ramon put his hand over Jake's mouth to make him quiet down. I scratched Ramon on his face and grabbed my son. Then I ran up the stairs to keep Jake away so I could deal with my husband.

He told me that since Jake was his son, he could do whatever he wanted to him. I told him no, that he would never touch him like that again, as I stood in front of the door, preventing Ramon from entering the room and going after Jake.

Ramon made it clear that he didn't want the baby because the doctor had told him that she could be born with Down syndrome. Then he grabbed me and tossed me down the stairs. Falling felt like minutes as I held my stomach to protect my baby girl. Once I made it down the stairs, I ran to the dining room and hid under the table.

He threw the dining set across the room, pushed me to the ground, and started kicking me all over. When I screamed and cried, he turned more aggressive, so I kept quiet, did my best to protect my stomach, and let him beat me. He finally got tired and walked away. I just lay there, grabbing my tummy, telling my unborn baby girl that I was sorry and that I had done my best to protect her.

I went upstairs to be with my son and lay on the bed with him as I cried as quietly as possible so Ramon would not hear me and become enraged again. I started collecting all my hair that was falling out, wadding it into a ball next to me. When I got up a short while later, he accused me of trying to set him up by saving my hair. I told him I wasn't, but he didn't believe me and ordered me to take a shower while he put the clothes I had been wearing in a bag.

Ramon grabbed the vacuum and started cleaning all around the bed, dining room, stairs, and wherever he had dragged me by my hair. After he was finished, he took the vacuum bag and tossed it in the other bag with my clothes. He told me to go to bed and then went outside to check around and see if the neighbors were looking outside. He was acting like my mother when she was covering her tracks. He was paranoid.

He left with the bag of hair and vacuum dust after that and came back twenty minutes later. I didn't know where he had gone, but I was listening to the front door for his return. My heart was pounding, my breathing faint—all I wanted was for him to just disappear forever. I hated not knowing what was coming next. I lay there just listening to every step he took, waiting for whatever was about to happen.

Then I heard him grab something from the fridge and flick the TV on. I was relieved and hoped he would just fall asleep on the couch. I was still too scared to fall asleep, so I just lay there listening to him watch some Spanish series until I eventually passed out.

I couldn't remember the last time I had a good night's sleep. First, it was my stepfather coming into my room and molesting me for years, then it was my mother dragging me out of bed by my hair in the middle of the night, and now this guy—my husband—was forcing me to protect my children from him. The familiar nightly hell was my way of life, I suppose, and every noise left me scared. Trying to sleep was exhausting for me because I had to work so hard at staying alert all the time. I was always half awake. I guess you can say I slept with one eye open. This was a normal way of life from the time I could remember.

A week or so after that, he told me to get ready because we needed to file the documents required to finish the process of "fixing" his papers. I got Jake ready and packed a bag for the day because I knew we would be in line for hours.

Our number was finally called, and we paid the final filing fee, but they told Ramon there was still more he needed to do in order to complete the process. Since he had been handling this whole situation, it was not clear to me what we hadn't done. He became very agitated, and we left quickly. As soon as we got in the car, it seemed too quiet.

Once we pulled onto the freeway, he began to degrade me, calling me garbage and telling me that I was nothing. He regretted marrying me because I was not able to keep him in the US. After yelling at me for a bit, he suddenly started screaming like crazy. When I told him to calm down because Jake was in the back seat, he punched me in the stomach with his right fist. I covered my stomach so he couldn't hit me again, and then he went for my hair, grabbing it and slamming my head into the window. He kept calling me white trash, and he kept repeating it.

I was afraid we were going to crash, and something would happen to Jake because every time Ramon hit me, the car swerved all over the road. A man pulled over and rolled down his window to yell at us, but I couldn't make out what he was saying. I just wished he would call the police. I looked into the back seat and thought to myself, *How is this kid still asleep?* I was relieved in a sense, though, because if Jake were crying, Ramon would have gotten even madder.

When he finally started to calm down, I thought to myself that I had to make him happy somehow. I kept quiet and stared out the window.

I started to talk more calmly to him after that day, and he seemed to like that. I did everything he told me to do without talking, and I did things the way he wanted them done. I'd make his dinner, attend to whatever he needed so that he would stay calm, and give him beer until he passed out. The house was so peaceful when he was sleeping. I wished he would stay drunk and pass out all the time so I wouldn't have to worry about him barging into the bathroom while I took a shower to yell at me over something he was angry about.

Finally, a letter from the immigration department came in the mail, and I was excited to see if they had made an appointment for him to get his papers. I thought fixing his papers would change him into a better man. Maybe this was a way for him to see that someone was answering his prayers. We had to wait a month until his appointment. During that period of time, he was caring and acted like a good father to our son. When he came home from work, he did not take his frustrations out on me. I was in heaven. I believed my prayers had been answered and that I would have no more pain, emotionally or physically.

On the way there, Ramon was so happy, talking about his future in the USA. At that moment, I thought he had become a better man—I was on cloud nine! As we sat in the waiting room, I felt my little girl moving around inside my belly. I was so thankful that this day had come. Just maybe Ramon would stop abusing me, and our lives would change for the better.

When Ramon was called into the interview room, security told me to wait right where I was. I didn't question them, so I just sat back down and waited a good hour, almost falling asleep in my chair before the sound of the door startled me, and I heard my name—not just any name though. They called me by my birth name, "Jessica Williams."

I asked them where my husband was, and they told me that he was being deported. Apparently, the law had been looking for him because he had sexually assaulted a minor in another state and had abused his girlfriend in another. He was moving from state to state, trying to dodge the police, and they told me I was just another one of his victims. I was in complete shock and did not understand.

I had to sit down and take it all in for a minute. I didn't know how to depend on myself. What was I going to do? All I could think was "How is this happening?" I'd never had freedom before, and I sat there so afraid, wondering how I was going to survive and support my children. I was pregnant with a one-year-old at home.

The immigration staff told me to be careful whom I marry next time. They didn't care, nor did they offer me any help at all! I called the babysitter who was watching my son to come pick me up because, even though I had the car, I didn't know how to drive home. She came to pick me up, and all I wanted was to hold Jake and never let him go.

I thought about my son and how he would take the news. There was also the future of my baby girl, who was about due—Ramon would not see her birth. I felt guilty because I was unable to fix his papers, and I knew he was going to be angry with me because of it. I had all these thoughts about my family, but I never thought about myself or how I was free from him. It never crossed my mind. I just felt helpless.

When I got home, I just looked around the house at all his things. It was so quiet. I had a meltdown and cried. I was so upset with myself because I felt as if this was my fault. Everything had always been my fault my whole life, so I emotionally beat myself up about this too. My son and my unborn baby girl weren't ever going to see their father again. I felt that my kids would be angry with me because they had no father.

That night was the first night I was able to make dinner and not freak out that Ramon wouldn't like it and would toss it across the room. It was a nice, quiet dinner with my son. We ate together in peace for once, without that man trying to force-feed Jake. The next morning when I woke up, I thought it had all been a dream. I went downstairs to check, but this was reality. He was gone.

The phone rang later in the morning, and I answered a collect call from the police department. My heart dropped as I accepted it. He still had complete control over me, as if he were still in the house. I was scared he would yell at me about what had happened at the immigration office, so when I answered the phone, I waited for him to say the first word.

"Hello," he said in his calm, quiet voice, that voice he used when he needed something. He was smart and knew if he were demanding and abusive over the phone, I would hang up. I just said, "Okay," to everything he asked of me. He told me that he loved me and didn't want me to take his kids away because we were a family. He needed me to bail him out of jail, find him a lawyer, and take good care of his son.

I felt angry, yet at the same time, I was sad for him. I thought of Jake and how he would feel if he were not able to see his father again. I stood there wishing I had a mother, father, sister, brother, friend, or even stranger, for advice, but I had no one except this man. I was completely alone with the decisions I had to make.

I cried my eyes out that day, knowing I had to be strong for my son and that my baby girl was due in just three weeks. I thought of him telling me that he would change and become a better man. His voice haunted me throughout the day. All I heard were his empty promises over and over again. I wanted to believe him. I wanted to see with my own eyes whether he would change for our family. I thought, *What if I missed the opportunity to see him change? What if I left too soon and didn't give him that one last chance?* That would make me a bad person, wouldn't it?

Chapter 12

Brainwashing

THE NEXT MORNING, HE DID NOT MAKE a collect call from jail; he called me from Costa Rica. He told me to sell all our things, go to Costa Rica, and fix his papers so we could all come back to the US together as a family. He kept telling me how much he loved me and his son and how he wished he could be with me during the birth of our baby girl.

My heart ached, and I felt sick because, deep down inside, I knew he couldn't be trusted. I knew he was just trying to get us down there so he could control me and stop me from leaving him. But I kept thinking to myself that if I didn't go, I would never know for sure whether he would change, and if I didn't know for sure, then I would live the rest of my life with regret.

So I started to sell his things and send him money so he could survive down there and shopped at Goodwill for clothing for our children.

I went to a doctor's appointment a week or so later to check on the baby and found out she was in a breech position. The doctor told me to send my son out of the room with a nurse because what they were about to do was going to be painful, and they didn't want to scare him.

They strapped my head, arms, and legs down onto the bed. I was terrified, knowing it was going to be extremely painful. They told me to take a deep breath and breathe out as they turned my baby around by massaging my stomach hard. I can't even describe the pain I endured. It felt as if they reached up inside me and were trying to rip her out. I wanted to pass out. I felt a big pop, and then they were done. The baby's head was now facing down, and she was safe to be delivered naturally.

I lay there with tears running down my face, wishing I would have just had her right then with all the pain I was in. As I walked to the bus stop, I was still in pain but glad my son had not witnessed what the doctor just did to me. I had a feeling I was going into labor but thought the feeling would pass, so we went home, and I laid Jake down for his nap.

I took a bath after that, thinking the pain would eventually stop, but it didn't. I lay down with my son, trying my hardest to relax my body, but I found myself becoming angry as I prayed. I asked God why he was putting me through so much pain and prayed for the agony to stop. I got in the shower again, hoping that would do the trick.

"Jessica! Where are you?" yelled a voice that belonged to my mother. She burst into the bathroom and ripped the shower curtain open to yell at me. I covered my naked body, yelling back at her to stop. She was so angry though; she was mad at my sister and wanted me to care for her because she was fed up.

She didn't even care that I was trying to avoid premature labor with my second child. She slapped me in the face and tried to punch me in the stomach, but I blocked her by catching her hand. I stood up to my mother, looking her dead in the eyes. I told her that she would never lay a hand on my baby again, or I would kick her out of my house.

She laughed and told me the thing in my belly was not a baby yet because she had not been born. I was so angry I pushed her out of the bathroom. "What are you doing?" she screamed. She was in shock because that was the very first time in my life that I had ever laid a hand on her. I'd never fought back before, but now it wasn't about me—it was about my child. I was amazed at myself for how mad I got with her that day.

My mother started pulling her hair out and slapping her own face like she always did when she freaked out. When she came toward me, I pushed her away and saw her fall down the stairs as if in slow motion. I went downstairs to see if she was okay, but she kept screaming, "You wanted to kill me!" I repeatedly told her it was her fault, that she was the one going crazy, but she kept ripping out her hair and slapping herself in the face.

That was what she hated hearing the most, being told she was acting crazy. I threw her out of my house and told her she was never allowed back again. She was screaming and crying as I closed the door. My sister continued to say she didn't want to leave with our mother. I asked her what she was planning to do then because I was in labor, and she said she wanted to stay with me.

I called a taxi to take me to the hospital, but when the nurse checked me, she said I was not dilated enough to be admitted. After I told her how much pain I was in, she said, "This is why kids should not have kids. They can't take the pain." I informed her that I already had a son and that the pain I was feeling was not normal, but she still sent me home.

Soaking in the bathtub was my only relief. I even fell asleep there for about two hours. My butt hurt because I had lain in the tub for so long!

In the morning, I called the babysitter to watch my son while I went back to the hospital, hoping this time I would be dilated enough to deliver. I did not want to leave Jake for that long and wished I would deliver and be able to go home the same night. She drove me to the hospital so I wouldn't have to pay for a taxi. When I got there, I threw up everywhere from the amount of pain I was in. Finally, they gave me some painkillers, and I started to feel relief.

Vanessa came into my hospital room a short while later. I was so happy she was there, and I did not have to be alone. I was ready to start pushing at that point, and the nurse went out to get things ready and contact the doctor. Then my mother came into the room, and I felt sick to my stomach all over again.

I was hoping she would be nice to me since I was having a baby, her second grandchild, but she slowly came to my side while glaring at me with an evil stare. As I lay on the hospital bed in stirrups, she spoke in her sick, sweet way, telling me she hoped I'd go through the hell I had put her through. She kept saying nasty things to me, that she would never visit the kids, etc. I was in so much pain I just wanted her to leave and did my best to block her out. The sounds coming from her mouth started to become muffled as I tried my best to concentrate on my baby. She lingered by my bedside, though, digging at me and repeating the same horrible things over and over.

Finally, I'd had enough, and I ordered her out, and Vanessa backed me up by telling her to get out too. My doctor got to the room and asked me if I was okay. I told her to make my mother leave, but before the doctor could do anything, my mother said she was leaving anyway. I knew she was glaring at me as she walked out of the room, and I just looked away and started to cry.

The doctor brought my mind back to what was most important at that moment, delivering a healthy baby. She told me to push, so I did. After two pushes, I passed out, and when I woke up, I thought I was at home, just sleeping in my bed. Then I realized I was at the hospital. I told myself to stay strong and stay awake for my child, so I continued to push, but she wasn't coming out—my energy was gone.

I lay there thinking about the things my mother had said, the fact that the father of my baby wasn't there, and my worries about my son crying because I was not with him. I was emotionally drained by those thoughts and the thoughts of how I was going to take care of my kids. I passed out again, later waking to see the doctor with a vacuum she was going to use to suck my baby out. I didn't want my baby hurt by it and told her to stop. She yelled at me to keep pushing, so I tried my hardest. Then finally, I felt a pop and a burning sensation. My baby girl was here!

She came out with big, beautiful eyes, looking all about the room. She had thick black hair and tan skin. For a second, I thought that could not possibly be my child because my son had come out bald and whiter than white, like a snowflake. I didn't hear her cry and began to worry because they kept wiping her and shaking her little body to get her to cry. A small cry finally came from the tiny lungs, and it was the cutest cry I would ever hear. I had never heard a baby give such a girly cry.

They put her naked body on my chest, and she latched on to my breast like a pro while making the cutest grunting noise. Vanessa was in tears, telling me she was the most beautiful baby she had ever seen. I had never seen my sister so emotional in my life; it was a selfless and pure moment we shared together. I decided to name my little girl Emilce, a pretty Spanish name that means "brave woman"—I figured she would need to be brave in the world we were living in. Nothing else mattered at that point. My job was to protect Emilce and Jake with all I had because I wasn't going to give anyone the opportunity to hurt the family I had made.

I stayed at the hospital overnight. When I picked up Emilce, I smelled her little head and prayed like I had never prayed before. I asked God to watch over us because I knew we had a struggle ahead. I asked him to protect us from harm, to see us through the dark times, and to give me the strength I needed to protect them from all the horrible people in the world.

Morning came, and I filled out all the necessary paperwork. I went through all the health exams before our release from the hospital. I had never been away from my son that long before, and we were both excited to see each other again. When he realized that I had Emilce with me, he was confused at first and looked at her. I explained to him that we were taking his new sister home, and he started smiling.

I just wished that I had a secure home and life to provide them both with because I had no idea what was going to happen next. Vanessa went to live with our mother after that, and I went on with my current situation. While I was doing the dishes, I had a complete meltdown and cried my eyes out, not knowing what to do. I was so confused, an emotional wreck. I had to stay positive for my kids, so I sucked it up. I had to think of what to do next.

Ramon called and asked how things were going. I told him I did not know if I was going to Costa Rica because I had just had the baby and wasn't ready to make that choice yet. He kept telling me what I wanted to hear and saying he was a changed man. He wanted to be a great father to the kids and pleaded with me not to take them away from him. I must admit it was working. I was feeling guilty like I was going to ruin the kids' lives if I took their father away.

I went to bed that night thinking about how this was the first time in my life I was alone, and I had two kids to take care of! It felt like a dream. It felt good to be alone, but at the same time, it was scary because I had never lived like that before. I had lived in fear since I was a child. I had never been given the opportunity to make my own choices and had never been away from someone who abused me. I was panicking to the point I felt like I was going into shock.

I pushed myself back to reality for the sake of my children because I knew I couldn't lose control. I denied everything. I told myself nothing was wrong and that those thoughts helped keep me together. I made a schedule for my kids to keep them as stable as possible; I wanted our situation to affect them as little as possible.

Ramon called me again, crying and begging me to sell the rest of our things and move to Costa Rica with him. My son had often asked about where he was, and I began to feel pity for the father of my children. Ramon made me feel guilty and told me that I was keeping his children from him. I didn't want to be that type of person because I was never able to see my father, and I knew how that affected me. I kept thinking about how I felt when I was a child, wishing my mother had not taken us away from our dad. I was so confused as to the right decision.

He kept telling me that he would be a better husband and father and that our family meant the world to him. He apologized for using drugs, saying that was the reason he was so terrible before. I had to make the hardest choice of my life that day. What if he did change? What if he did see his mistakes? What would happen if I took his kids away, not giving him another shot? I wondered if the kids would hate me one day for not trying just one last time.

Chapter 13

What Is the Right Choice?

I FINALLY DECIDED. I DID WHAT HE wanted me to do because I believed him, and I wanted to believe that my life and my kids' lives could get better. I made the choice to sell everything and move to Costa Rica. He asked me to bring a few of his personal things he'd left behind, like music CDs, movies, pictures, and clothes. Buying the airfare took most of the money I had saved up, leaving me with a few hundred dollars.

I said goodbye to my grandpa and a few of my friends. One of my friends asked me, "What makes you think he won't hurt you over there?" and told me I was making a big mistake, but I assured him that I had a two-way ticket to come back in two weeks if Ramon didn't really change. I had to find out for myself because if I didn't go, then I would never know. This was something I had to do one last time. I told him I would call him if I needed him. I thought I had a safe way out if needed.

At the airport, reality set in, and I couldn't believe I was on my way to Costa Rica with two little kids. I wasn't sure about the feelings I was having though. I couldn't wait to see how beautiful it was over there, if there were lots of animals, what kind of food they ate, and where we would be living.

The excitement of a different culture had me curious, but a part of me knew I was doing the wrong thing. Why was I leaving to see the man who beat me, used me, and didn't want my kids? Part of me thought I was going to get myself killed and wondered, if I died, would anyone look for me? Was I putting my kids in danger? I shut my thoughts down and started to pretend that everything was going to be fine.

I was nervous about being high up in the air, but Jake was so happy to be in an airplane, and baby Emilce slept the whole ride with feedings often. The pilot announced that there was going to be some turbulence, so I grabbed my kids and prayed. I asked God to protect my kids and watch over them because, at that moment, I wasn't sure if I was going to die while we were in Costa Rica.

I closed my eyes and tried not to panic for my children's sake. I didn't want to scare them. I couldn't believe I was sitting there, accepting the fact that I knew we were going to die on our way down to Costa Rica. The plane felt like a roller-coaster ride, dropping up and down. Jake was having the time of his life because he thought it was just a fun ride!

Finally, the plane stopped shaking, and we were able to take off our seat belts and enjoy the rest of the ride in peace. Our dinner was horrible—all that money on plane tickets, and they couldn't even feed us something decent. I ate it anyway because I had no idea when I was going to eat again. People were commenting on how tiny the baby was, asking why I was bringing a tiny baby like that on the airplane. They looked at me like I was crazy when I told them we were visiting their father.

As I looked out the window, down at the ocean, I swear I could see the tops of whales. It looked like they were diving in and out of the sea with so much grace. I sat there looking at my kids, wondering for the millionth time if I was making the right choice.

I was doing this for my children so that they could have their father and we could be a family. I thought God would punish me if I didn't try because I married him and then just gave up. If I broke that promise I made when we married, it would be a sin. Even though I married to get out of my mother's abusive home, I still thought that way for some odd reason.

Before I knew it, we were in Costa Rica. My stomach started to feel sick as we made our landing. I was worried about how Ramon was going to react to his new baby girl, the one he didn't want. The air felt different once we got off the plane—humid and warm, with a different smell to it. I was shaking as I held my daughter and grabbed my son's hand while I looked for Ramon. I held on to my kids tightly. No way was I letting go!

Then I saw him, and I felt sick to my stomach all over again when he noticed me. I expected him to run up and hug us all, but he just kind of walked over and gave our son a hug. Jake was so happy to see his father again, but he was too young to understand how mean he was. In his two-year-old mind, he was having fun in a new place. I asked Ramon if he wanted to see his daughter, but the look in his eyes said no.

I uncovered the blanket anyway, thinking that her beautiful face would change his mind, but it did not. He didn't seem happy. He just looked at her and said that she looked like my mother. Then he asked me where his money and things were. I was so mad that he had no intention of holding his baby; all he cared about were his material things. I let him know that his things were still on the airplane and we needed to go to baggage claim to collect them. Then I handed him the rest of the money.

He looked stunned, and I felt my heart drop when he had that look of anger in his eyes. "Where the fuck is all the money?" he yelled out, right in the middle of the airport. I explained to him where it all went and how much the tickets had cost to get us all down there, but he pushed me and called me all kinds of names. I felt humiliated, as people were looking at us when they walked by.

I apologized over and over to him, telling him that I could bring back more after I went back to the US in two weeks because I had bought two-way tickets. He laughed at me and told me that I was not leaving without him. I couldn't believe it! I hadn't been in the country for an hour, and he was already the same as he had always been.

People were right about him not changing, and deep down inside, I had known too. I thought he would be thankful for what he had because we were a family, and now we were together again. It was not the greeting I had expected it to be, but in a way, I knew this was coming. This was just who he was. I had to see for myself, though, so I wouldn't live the rest of my life with regret.

I was so tired, hungry, and scared. My breasts were full of milk, and it was painful, so I just wanted to get somewhere safe to feed my baby. When we went to the baggage claim, I noticed that a box was missing, but no one spoke English, so I couldn't really communicate.

Thankfully, they finally found someone who spoke English and located the box of Ramon's things. It took us five hours to get to the house we would be living in, on the border of Costa Rica and Panama. I felt like the worst mother in the world for bringing my kids out there.

I must say, though, I had never seen a place more beautiful in my life. There were parrots flying in the sky from tree to tree, waterfalls, volcanoes, mountains, and rivers gushing with water—the smell was so fresh, the air so clean. I couldn't believe my eyes! I loved the fruit trees, mango, banana, guava, etc. I was so excited to explore this beautiful place that I forgot about the situation I was in for a moment.

Reality was back, and we pulled up to his father's house. All these people came out smiling and happy to see us, kissing us all on both cheeks. After they were done, I could smell their saliva on my face and got grossed out, but they were all very nice. Ramon completely changed the way he treated me around them, becoming a totally different person with his family. I saw him being nice for once, and I thought that maybe if I just did what he wanted and did it right, maybe he could change into this person. It seemed possible.

I was the sweetest I could be with him, pretending like everything had always been okay and he was being good back to us. We ate dinner with his family; it was so wonderful to see that they all had manners and such class. They cherished their meal like it was their last.

His father, Carlos, showed me his cows and the property, which was the size of a small village! He had a house every hundred yards, having built a home for each of his children. Carlos's house was a three-story home that was so clean, with no clutter, and had tile work throughout the whole house. As we walked through the property, I thought to myself that his father, sisters, and brothers were amazingly wonderful people with big hearts. They seemed like the kind of people who would give anyone the shirts off their backs.

I went outside and looked over a hill, where there was a big stream of water flowing fast down a path, and I stood out there listening to the peaceful atmosphere. I had never seen such beauty in nature; his place was truly paradise! Despite the beauty, I started to feel that sense of worry again. As I walked with my baby girl in my arms and my little boy by my side, I struggled with my emotions, wondering if this was the right choice and whether my children would be safe.

While we walked, Ramon still had not even held his daughter. His love for Jake was so sweet to me that it made me think I'd made the right choice by coming to Costa Rica, but I felt so alone and confused. At this point, I wasn't sure if I was dreaming or going completely insane. Part of me wished for him to change so we could be happy together; the other part of me wished I would wake up back in the US tomorrow like this had never happened.

We arrived at our cute little home sitting along the edge of the road. It was baby blue with a front porch. Across the road was a river that sounded beautiful as the water rushed down the stream. There were four different kinds of banana trees in the front yard, and in the back were yards of coffee bean plants that were harvested yearly. His family told me that was the time of year when the women got a chance to make money for clothes and things for the house or a vacation—almost like tax season in the US because they looked forward to the harvest all year. The men took care of the coffee crops all year long, and the women harvested the beans by tying baskets in front of them and picking the red-colored beans. It was like a competition among the women to pick the most beans since they were paid by how much the basket weighed—kind of interesting to watch. I tried a few baskets myself, and it was harder than it looked. Those women were amazing at picking coffee!

Chapter 14

Life in Costa Rica

I SETTLED INTO THE ONE-BEDROOM HOME WE were staying in and put everything I'd brought on the bed. I started feeling that sickness in my stomach again, wanting to lie down and rest, but not here. I wanted to go home, where everyone spoke English and I was understood. I put my kids to bed that night, mentally preparing myself for alone time with Ramon. I sat down on the kitchen bar and waited for him to make the first move. Looking at him made me sick, so I looked down at the floor and hoped he would just get it over with quickly so I could get some sleep.

The thing I worried about most was that he would want sex from me because he had been alone for a couple of months. I prepared my body and soul to block it out. Sure enough, as he approached me, I knew that was exactly what he wanted. I wished I could just run away and scream. I had this weird, disgusted feeling when he touched me. There was no kissing or romance at all with him, ever. I always closed my eyes and took my mind to another place. I would sing a song like I used to when my mother beat me, or I would think of the things I needed to do the next day. I couldn't even feel anything as he was just on top of me, moving up and down, only concerned about satisfying himself. When he was done, I had to get a rag and clean him up. I felt like a sex slave. I ended up feeling more numb than I ever had in my life.

I took my first shower in their country that night, and it was the worst shower I had ever taken. It was cold, and the shower space was as big as a room—five people could have fit in that shower at one time! There were strange wires connected to the shower to heat the water, but it was broken. I took a shower in freezing-cold water with no shampoo or conditioner. I had to use a bar soap to wash my hair, making it hard and difficult to brush. I just put it in a messy bun and went to bed.

At four in the morning, when it was still pitch dark outside, I was woken to learn how to wash laundry and make Costa Rican food. I was in disbelief, still so exhausted from our journey to this foreign land, and I could not even have a day or two to recuperate. Just as I finished getting ready, I heard a knock at the door, and I could not believe my eyes.

There stood five ladies who were all his sisters, and, one by one, they greeted me with a kiss on both cheeks as they walked in. I had never been greeted in such a manner! After the last sister walked in, I closed the door and stood there waiting for them to say something first, but we all just looked at each other and giggled.

We had no idea how to communicate, unable to speak each other's language, so I finally made the first move and headed to the kitchen to make something to eat. One of the sisters jumped into the kitchen and told me to sit down, not in English, of course, but she directed my body to a chair. I felt so weird because I had never sat down while someone cooked for me. I was always the one who cooked, cleaned, and entertained guests. I was afraid that if Ramon came home, he would be mad at me.

As I sat, I started to panic, with this urge to get her out of the kitchen and take over the cooking responsibilities, but I just sat there watching them. They cooked leftover beans and rice with eggs mixed in, and we ate it with French bread and coffee. When Jake woke up and was hungry, all five ladies were all over him like they had never seen a little boy before. They loved him because this was their nephew. I was happy they treated Jake with so much love.

After our meal, one of the sisters guided me to the back patio, where there was a large sink to wash clothes in. She showed me how to wash the clothes by hand. I had never seen clothes washed like that before, so I wasn't good at it! She was laughing at me because I was so grossed out by the dirty clothes in that nasty water.

She grabbed a shirt and threw it in the sink of soapy water, tossed it on this rock-looking thing, and started scrubbing like there was no tomorrow. After she was done, she tossed the shirt into some clean water and threw it into this machine. We both kept going until the clothes were done and the machine was full. When she turned it on, it spun the clothing to wring the water out of them. It was such a strange way to do laundry—I had never seen such a thing. Now they were all laughing at me because I was clueless about washing laundry by hand.

After the device was done spinning, she put all the clothes in a basket and showed me to the clothesline outside. I thought to myself, *You have got to be kidding me. After all that work, there is still more!* Back in the USA, I would have had all the clothes cleaned and put away by now. She had a cup full of clothing pins to hang everything on the line, showed me how to hang the laundry, and kept handing me clothes after that so I could hang them myself. By the time we were done, the line was full, and man, was I tired!

I went to the house to check on Emilce, who was still asleep. One of the sisters showed me where the bucket and sponge were, and I just wanted them to go away at this point. I followed her to watch where to fill the bucket with water. She started sweeping the floor, and soon after, there was a pile of dirt, which she scooped up with a dustpan. Then she started scrubbing the floor by hand on her knees.

After that, I moved to help her up, but she said, "No, no!" and grabbed a cream polish and showed me how to polish the tiles. She did one tile, and I did the rest. I had to do every inch of the room. When I finished, I was exhausted! This was not how we did things in the USA. I was so glad I had finished for the day, or so I thought.

I hadn't been sitting down long when another sister brought over food to make dinner; I guess my little break was over. I followed her to the kitchen, where she emptied the bags full of chicken and all kinds of veggies. I had a feeling I knew what she was going to make: chicken soup. She chopped up a whole chicken and tossed the pieces into a pot of water and added seasonings. As the chicken cooked, she made steamed rice and added the veggies to the pot as soon as it was done. It was a fast dinner, I thought.

Ramon came home and gave kisses to his sisters on both cheeks; it was weird for me to see him show affection like that, so I went to my room. He called out to me and asked if I had learned how to do all the house chores, and I said yes. His sisters served him his meal, and while he ate his dinner, I went outside to grab the clothes from the line. I couldn't believe they were dry already. I put the basket on the patio and began to fold laundry, completely drained from the day. As I put the things away, he asked me—nicely—for more soup. I wished he was nice like that to me all the time and wondered if he was changing.

Little Jake was so happy to see his father and wanted to play with him. Ramon told me he was going to take our son down the gravel road to his father's house. I didn't want him to go, but I really had no choice in the matter. I worried for my son while getting him ready to go. I asked him how long he would be, but he just told me that his other brothers wanted to meet our son. The house was not too far, so I calmed myself with the thought that if he was gone too long, I could just walk up there carrying Emilce.

The house was quiet and lonely; I sat there thinking of what the future held. I didn't really think about the language barrier I'd be facing when I came down there. I literally had no way of communicating with anyone around me except Ramon—that thought terrified me and made me feel like I had no way out. I started to see the reality of my current situation with my children, out in the middle of nowhere in a foreign land, and I was unable to go anywhere else.

I realized we were in trouble, and I needed to find a way to get us out of there. I did not want him to do anything to my daughter because I knew he did not want her—he still hadn't even held her! I knew I was going to do everything in my power to protect my children. I was their mother and had to make it for them.

Ramon finally came back with Jake. I was thankful but knew it was time to put the kids to sleep, and I knew what was next. I had to do my next job as his wife, which was having sex with him. As it was happening, I closed my eyes so I didn't have to look at him, but he kept telling me to look into his eyes. I just wanted to run away.

He never did last that long, so it was over before I knew it, and time to wipe him off and make sure he was clean. I realized I hated him with all my heart. Sometimes I would cry, but I did it silently, never letting him know because that would have given him a reason to hit me or mock me.

A few weeks passed, and I had finally gotten used to the schedule of waking up at four in the morning to make breakfast and lunch for Ramon to take to work. Then it was doing the laundry, scrubbing the house spotless, and making dinner. Sometimes I was so quick with my chores that I had enough time to go for walks with the kids before he got home from work. Little by little, we walked farther and farther. I began to enjoy the simple life and appreciate the smallest things. I got to know the people who lived around the town, but I would rush home to get dinner ready fast enough and make sure the laundry was put away before Ramon got back.

We had a doctor from town come and give immunizations to Emilce, who was two months old at the time. He spoke English, and I was confident that he was a good doctor. Ramon watched me as I spoke with the doctor because he didn't like me being "too friendly" with other men or finding a way to escape by telling him the truth about Ramon. I hated not being able to be myself, pretending life was perfect for his benefit. I knew I had to get to know people, but I also knew I had to obey the father of my children.

Chapter 15

Family Sunday Dinner

Dinner every Sunday was a big family meal at his father's house. No one works on Sundays in Costa Rica, apparently, and in Ramon's family, everyone got together and made dinner. They went to church in the mornings, and afterward, the women went home to prepare food while the men played soccer together.

Slowly, I started learning how to speak Spanish. I asked his sisters how to say simple things at first, like "fork" or "rice." Soon I began to speak to them in small sentences, but I kept it a secret from my husband because I knew he would be upset if I could communicate.

One day, after I was done with my long day of chores, I went for a walk with the kids and saw the most awesome thing ever: a sloth! I could not believe my eyes. I started crying, and my son was confused. I told him what it was, and he just wanted to pet it because he was curious as to why it was so low to the ground. I tried to pick him off the tree, but he wouldn't let me hold him. He appeared to be injured, and I wanted to take him home. I tried for an hour, but he wouldn't budge, so I left him there, praying he would climb higher so other animals wouldn't eat him.

I felt good about seeing something new for a change. On the walk back home, I wanted to tell Ramon about what we had seen and how exciting it was, but I didn't think it was a good idea for him to know we were exploring. We never had real conversations together; he always just ordered me around or told me how to do things his way.

I finally had something to look forward to though: finding new things to see! Every day, after I finished my chores, we went in search of something interesting that we had not seen yet. One time, I went up a hill that was so big I almost turned around because I didn't want Ramon to get home before I did. I didn't want him to know I was out, or he would have gotten mad. At the top, I stood there blinking my eyes, not believing what I was seeing: the indigenous people of Costa Rica. There was a little village of them, with tepees they lived in and firepits they cooked on. Most of them were naked. There were a lot of children playing and adults working the land. It was like a scene from a movie. I had no idea people like this still existed. It was unreal but amazing.

I hurried home down the hill, changed into my pajamas quickly, and then made dinner. After he came home and finished eating, he watched the news every night—that was his routine. I cleaned the dishes and went to bed.

The next day was Sunday when he played soccer, and his sisters made plans to cook with the other women. That day, they made a big pot of soup with rice, and some women made fried pork with cabbage salad, while others made this root that they only cooked once a year. The root was yellow, and they ground it up and boiled it until it was soft. Then they put it in nylon to drain out the water, and after it was dry enough, they fried it and served it along with the pork and salad. It was good with the spicy vinegar they made. I had never had such good food in my life.

On my way home, I listened to the CD I had brought with me, the *Waiting to Exhale* soundtrack. I even had the movie with me as well. I sang to the soundtrack often and watched the movie repeatedly like they were my friends and I was their friend with a bad relationship. I felt like we were all working together to make it out, and that soundtrack gave me hope. I danced and laughed with the kids, but then he would come home, and the fun stopped because I had to pretend that my life was all for him.

Chapter 16

Waking Up in a Barn

It wasn't long before the beauty of my surroundings became the background of my abuse—things got bad fast! Ramon wanted his papers fixed, and it was my fault they weren't. He became more and more annoyed until he exploded on me one day.

That day, he slapped me in the face and started pulling my hair, threw me to the ground, and kicked me all over my body. The kids were screaming and crying while I begged him to stop. Emilce was five months old at the time. I told him I would do anything he wanted, cook him anything, whatever he wanted—just please stop. When I tried to comfort my children, he grabbed a pan from the kitchen and hit me in the head with it.

I woke up in the barn out back, where he kept all his work supplies. I was tied up with yellow rope. I was terrified that he had done something to the children and felt like I was going crazy. I just screamed. Not knowing what may or may not have happened to them was the worst feeling ever; all these thoughts came to mind. I wanted to protect Jake and Emilce, but I couldn't. I knew his brother lived nearby, so I screamed as loud as I could, but he must have been a football field away.

Ramon burst into the barn and told me that if I didn't shut up, he would kill me. My heart sank because I knew he would. He told me how much he hated me and how I was garbage. I could hear the kids crying inside. I had to comfort them and breastfeed my daughter. I had to figure out how to get him to let me go. I thought to myself, *Every man likes sex*, so I offered him oral sex. He looked at me like I was a stranger. I had never initiated sex with him before; he had always forced himself upon me.

I told him everything he wanted to hear. I told him I realized I had been a bad wife and should treat him better. It made me sick inside, but I said it with pure confidence. I just wanted to comfort my kids and would do anything to be near them. He got a thrill out of me begging to have sex with him. He looked so proud of himself. I took that opportunity to ask him if I could see the kids and put them to bed first, and he said I could.

I couldn't show him my happiness. I just walked up to the back door holding his hand, thanking him for allowing me back inside. I didn't care what I had to do to him later; I had my kids back. Their scent, Jake's voice, Emilce's cry, and the feeling of their hair were the most beautiful things ever. I laid Jake down for bed and then breastfed Emilce, gazing into her eyes while she looked at mine. I knew I would do whatever it took not to let that happen again. I had to please him in every way. I felt as if I had given up on myself.

After the kids fell asleep, I put on a sexy outfit, pretending I was someone else. He lay there waiting for me on the sofa, I gave him a lap dance, and he indicated he was ready for what I owed him. I had to have sex and do it right so he would know how much I appreciated his gratitude for letting me back in the house.

When we were done, he asked what had come over me because I had been acting completely different, but he liked me better that way. After he went to sleep, I lay there sick to my stomach, thinking about how emotionally exhausted I was. I had to keep up with pretending to accept this abuse. I wanted to go back home to the US, but how? I couldn't leave without my kids, and he would never let me just take them. Then I started to think the worst. I looked at him with disgust and hatred, wanting to kill him. I thought about how easy it would be to do it and just get rid of him once and for all.

Days went by, and I played loud music and danced all around the house with my kids as if I had hope. It was an outlet of some sort. He began to see how much more attentive to him I was sexually. What he didn't know was that I was secretly planning an escape with the kids. Weeks went by, and I never lost sight of freedom.

Whenever we had sex, killing him felt more and more like the right thing to do. I kept a knife in the room, and as he slept, I realized how easy it would have been to stab him because he had no chance of fighting back. I thought hard about what to do, knowing if I made a mistake, there would be no turning back. He would kill me and then the kids or kill me and raise them to be like him.

That night, after the kids fell asleep, he was on the sofa, watching the news. I asked God if he could send me a sign—was this the right thing to do? I was confused and upset at the thought that it had come to this. Was I about to kill the father of my children? My future played out inside my head, repeatedly, about how I was going to do it without him fighting back. I didn't care that I was about to kill him. I just didn't want him to attack me or hurt the children if I didn't do it right.

If I had killed him, his family would never have let me out of the country. Surely I would have ended up in a foreign jail without my children. After all the abuse I had gone through throughout my life, this was as low as I got. I never wanted to harm anyone as much as I wanted to end this man's life. He was a threat to my children, so I was in protective mode. I just couldn't snap out of it, but I realized that having my kids in my life was much more important than killing an evil man, so there had to be another way.

I prayed hard that night, asking to save my soul from the thought of killing my husband. I wanted to be free from the evil life I was living, and I made a deal with the man above: if he would help me protect my kids, then I would let him guide me out of this situation. From that day on, I spoke to God as if he was my friend like he was sitting on a bench beside me, and I blocked out all the evil thoughts and evil doings of my husband, soaking in the small blessings he brought every day.

Ramon continued to notice changes in me, asking me once again to explain why I was being different. I asked him if he believed in God. He said he did not because, if there were a god, then he would have given him a wife to fix his papers. I could not hold back my tongue at his insult and said to him, "God does not give blessings to evil people." It was the wrong thing to say at that time.

He punched me so hard that I fell to the ground, and he continued to beat me badly that day. Then his sisters came to the door, yelling at him to open it. When he finally did, he ordered me to the room. They came inside and asked where I was. He said I was sleeping, but his sister knew something was wrong, so she opened the bedroom door.

I was standing there with my face badly bruised. It was the moment I had dreamed that someone would find out about the abuse. My hair was falling out from being freshly beaten, and she grabbed me and yelled at him. He kept telling her to leave him alone and for me to go back to the room.

He went to his father's house that night and left me with the kids. I sat there fixing my hair and taking out the pieces that were already falling out. There were bumps all over my head, and I regretted not having the courage to kill him.

CHAPTER 17

My Sweet Baby Girl Was Sick

EMILCE WAS SEVEN MONTHS OLD WHEN I noticed one day that she had a fever. I kept a worried eye on her all night. Ramon did not speak to me that night. He just lay down and went to bed, so I was thankful he had not asked me for anything. My daughter was getting warmer by the minute, not eating anything because she couldn't keep my breast milk down.

Morning came, and I felt like it took days for the sun to come up. After Ramon woke up, I told him that Emilce was sick and I needed to take her to the hospital. He told me it was my fault, and if she died, it would be on me. All I wanted to do was run out of the house because I was so upset! I stayed up all night trying to think of a way to leave him and go to the hospital with both of my children.

I remembered that the bus came every day, once a day. I needed money, though, and I saw his wallet on the counter with all the other junk he kept in his pocket. I looked at the bedroom and could still hear him snoring. I was scared to lay one finger on his stuff, let alone open his wallet and take money, but I had to get my baby to the hospital.

It was a risk I was willing to take; I took a deep breath and grabbed it. He had a bit of money in his wallet, so I took from the center to avoid it looking like any was missing. I put the money in my purse and went to bed, not getting a minute of sleep. I was so scared he would catch me.

Ramon never asked how his daughter was doing in the morning. He just ate his breakfast, took his lunch, and went off to work like any other morning. After I saw him leave to work in the coffee fields, I checked on Emilce, who was hot and very weak. I thought to myself, *I am doing this, and nothing will stop me.*

I packed a bag with clothes and a few other things, but I didn't have our IDs or passports; Ramon had taken those upon arrival. I took what I could, grabbed my kids, and walked to the bus stop. Thoughts of panic ran through my head the whole way there. What if he came home early and I wasn't there? What if someone saw me and asked where I was going? I looked down at my baby, and she looked almost dead. I had to get to the hospital fast!

When the bus came and we boarded, I just handed the driver all the money I had. I had no idea how much Costa Rican money was worth, and he looked at me like I was crazy for giving him all that money. A lady on the bus spoke English and told me that the hospital was three hours away. He counted out what was needed for the fare to the nearest city, which was San José.

The city was huge, but luckily for me, there were enough people who spoke English to guide me to the hospital. A doctor rushed to my aid as soon as I got there, taking my very sick little girl from me for treatment. I was relieved yet scared at the same time; he told me that hundreds of children had been coming in with a deadly virus.

I thought at first that he said the word "deadly" because his English was broken, but he was right. There was a deadly virus, and there was a room full of crying mothers whose kids had the same illness as Emilce. We were all there in the room with our children, who all had IVs put in to hydrate them from all the vomiting and diarrhea. They were all losing weight so fast. I soon forgot about Ramon and wasn't scared anymore because I was in public and around others.

Days went by, and there were still no signs of her getting better. I was terrified because children were dying left and right, but I had to stay strong for both of my children. Jake kept me busy as we both waited there patiently for some sign of improvement, but Emilce was so skinny, and her hair was falling out. It was hard to look at her with tubes in her little nose and IVs in her tiny hands, wondering if I would be the next mother to have her daughter die. I was so angry with myself for even giving him another chance. All I wanted to do was go back to the USA.

A week later, one of the doctors told me that a man was looking for me and his kids. I told him the truth, the first time I had spoken out to someone who could help me. I told him that my husband was abusive, that I was leaving him, and that I did not want him around my children. The doctor made him leave, and I was so happy and thankful to have someone to protect us from him.

After that, I was too scared to take Jake for walks around outside. I felt bad that he was all cooped up in that hospital. For a two-year-old boy, he did very well. I promised him that I would get them out of that country and away from their father. I had made the mistake of going there to show Ramon that his daughter was not disabled and that she was a healthy girl. I wanted him to see her with love. He was still abusive, and I hated him. I knew then I was done, once and for all.

We spent three long months in the hospital, sleeping on small mats or rocking chairs; I had gotten used to sleeping sitting up. I started to see Emilce gradually get better to the point I was able to breastfeed her again—thankfully, I was still producing milk.

That night, I had a dream that I was walking in the woods, and a bright light hovered over the kids and me, shining so brightly that it was all I could see. I felt the presence of a higher being, and that scared me. I thought it was there to punish me, so I got on my knees and begged it to just take me. I wanted my kids to live a good life I never had. I felt a strong, peaceful vibe and looked up to see my kids and me standing there without their father. I felt like it was trying to tell me it was okay to leave Ramon.

I woke up extremely thankful that we were all still there. That day, it turned out Emilce was getting better faster, and in a week, we would be able to leave. I was so happy that everything was going to be okay with her health, but what was I going to do now? Where would we go from there? Where was home?

I told the doctor about Ramon taking our passports, and he directed me to the US Embassy. I called the office from the hospital and explained what had happened; they asked me so many questions! I went in for a fingerprint scan, and they told me it would take at least five months to get our passports, and even then, I still did not have the money to pay for airfare back. They even gave me a fine for overstaying in Costa Rica—I couldn't believe it!

Ramon's father, Carlos, was at the hospital when I got back from the embassy. I did not want to talk to him, and it didn't really matter because he didn't speak English, but the doctor said he would translate.

Carlos apologized for his son's actions. I had never seen a man cry as hard as he did that day. I didn't think anyone knew or cared, and I never expected to hear an apology from anyone. He told me to go home, back to the United States, but I misunderstood him at first. I thought he meant to go home with him, back to Ramon. He handed me money to buy plane tickets and gave us our passports, and I even had enough to pay the fine the embassy had given me. I was so relieved! I gave him the biggest hug. The feeling of freedom was so amazing I couldn't even explain it—you would have to feel it yourself to understand.

I met a lawyer at the hospital, and she let us stay at her house for a few weeks. She and her family were nice and helped me get the things I needed to return to the USA. We made it to the airport, and I had only one bag of belongings, a few pairs of clothes for the kids and diapers. I was so grateful for the help of people I did not know. I found out that people who are not friends or family are more willing to help.

I had left my photo album with all the pictures and memories in the kids' clothing and toys at Ramon's house. I knew I would never get them back, and I did not care as long as I had my kids and we were able to break free. Those items were the only thing Ramon received from us because we were not coming back.

Chapter 18

Freedom at Twenty-One

WHEN WE BOARDED THE PLANE, READY FOR takeoff, I was overwhelmed with joy. I held my little girl in my arms and held my son's hand as we started our journey back to US soil. I was not even afraid of the flight this time; I completely forgot that I feared heights. An hour into the flight, Jake asked where his dad was—he wanted to see him. I knew his little mind didn't comprehend the situation we had all been through. I felt so sorry for him, but I knew leaving was for his own good.

When we finally landed, I called the only person I knew in that area, my sister Vanessa. I told her I was back and needed a place to stay. She was sixteen at the time, which meant that my mother had to drive her to get us and that I was going to be living under her roof again. Obviously, I wasn't looking forward to this at all, but I had no other choice. It was better than staying in Costa Rica.

My mother hadn't changed a bit and had set up a list of rules for me if I was going to stay there:

1. No kids in the house after 4:00 a.m., which meant I had to get them up and ready so we were out the door by 4:00 a.m.

2. No kids eating in her kitchen, eating her food, or making any mess whatsoever.
3. No kids walking around her house annoying her.

I was walking on eggshells again, afraid my kids might make her angry. I felt angry leaving every morning while it was dark out with two little kids who had no idea why they had to leave their grandmother's house so early. I held my daughter in my arms and had Jake by the hand. Walking down the block, I thought to myself that this was going to be another long road ahead and pondered where we could go for the day without a car, on foot, with two small children. How would I feed them today?

I remembered the welfare office and found the nearest business to direct me to the local office. I waited outside for hours for them to open; I was first in line that day. I told them my whole situation and that we had just gotten back from Costa Rica. They checked our passports and found out I was telling the truth. I explained that we were staying with my mother now but had no diapers, food, or bus fare so I could find a job.

They understood my situation and gave me the help I needed. I was so thankful. I got diapers and food stamps for that month while my case was being processed. Then they gave me a bus pass for the month so I could find a job. They paid for my kids' day care while I worked. It was almost too good to be true. The welfare office helped me in a way that no one ever had, and for that, I am eternally grateful.

That night, we returned to my mother's house tired, and the kids were crying. All we wanted was a warm bed to sleep in, so I snuck into my room as quietly as possible and went straight to bed. My mother came into the room and flicked the light on, glaring at me with those green eyes of hers. She told me I had to find a place as soon as possible because she was not happy with having me there. I said, "Okay," and she flicked the light off and left. Trust me, I was relieved. I was not going to be staying in that dysfunctional house for long.

I kept everything I was doing during the day to myself because I knew my mother all too well; she would find some way to sabotage my success. I got out of her house on time every morning and worked as hard as I could to get on my feet. There was a feeling of insecurity inside me still though. No matter what anyone had done to hurt me, I was more scared to be alone than when I dealt with their abuse.

I knew it was going to take some time to get over all the abuse, but I did not understand how painful it would be to go through those emotions. Everywhere I went, I felt anxious and scared with no one to turn to. I was afraid to trust anyone, even myself, to make the right decisions.

After a long day of job hunting, as I sat in my room watching my kids sleep, I wondered when I was going to make the first step to leave this abusive life once and for all. Was I ever going to do it? I left Ramon, so why couldn't I leave my mother now? I knew she was going to hurt my children sooner or later, and I knew more than likely that would happen if I did not make the choice to leave. My heart was beating so fast, and my mind was racing with all these thoughts at once when it finally hit me. I had this strong urge to leave and told myself, "I am doing it. I am leaving first thing in the morning."

I packed all our things that fit inside a duffel bag. I wanted to just leave it all behind, but the kids needed their clothing and diapers. I cleaned the room and made the bed as a thank-you for letting me stay at her house. I showed the utmost respect even though she hated me with passion. When morning came, I loaded my kids up in the stroller.

My mother saw me with all my things and started yelling at me, "Where are you going?" while trying to snatch my bags from me.

I pulled them back and headed for the door, saying, "I'm leaving!"

She started screaming even louder, "What? You think you're too good to live with me?" She followed outside to the middle of the road and started screaming and pulling out her hair. I didn't understand why she was acting like that when she wanted me to leave.

I just kept walking away while pushing the double stroller down her street. She was yelling and crying with so much agony. I wanted to look back but told myself, "Just keep going. You're almost out." I kept walking down that long road to freedom. Something amazing happened. I soon heard my own two feet walking the road and the sweet sounds of Jake and Emilce. I could not hear the screams of my mother anymore, and to me, that felt so amazing. At that moment, I knew we were free from all the drama. I had help from welfare and a stroller for the kids. All I needed was to keep moving forward and make better choices in people.

We got to the BART station, and it came down to the next decision, and this was an easy one: where were we going to go? I looked at the map on the wall, and we took BART to Oakland, California. I liked living there as a kid. Oakland High was one of the best schools I had attended. I knew it was the best choice as long as we were far from my mother.

I got to Oakland, and I just sat at the public bus bench guarding my children as they slept. I felt like a paranoid mother observing everyone in sight. I knew I needed sleep, but I also knew it was not safe. Never in my life had I seen so many drug dealers! They kept coming up to me and asking me if I wanted to buy from them. I couldn't imagine what my life would be like if I did drugs!

I wanted to get off the streets to somewhere safe, and I noticed the bridge, which seemed warmer and more secluded than being in front of everyone who passed down the street. I went up and under the bridge and felt higher and safer. The only thing I was panicking about was the cars driving past the bridge. I felt a vibration as the cars passed the bridge and felt as if it were going to fall on top of us.

I bought food at a market using food stamps the next day, and I washed us up in the store restroom. We went to a nearby park for a picnic so we could eat lunch and I could think about my next move. I sat there watching my kids play, not knowing where to begin, feeling as if I couldn't do it all alone. I just did what I knew needed to be done at that moment. I pushed my kids on the swing set and began to smile, and that made me feel better.

Later in the day, while we were at the bus stop, a man asked me if we needed a place to stay. I didn't know what to say. He said he'd noticed me and the kids at that bus stop for a few days, and we looked as if we needed help. He was an absolute stranger coming out of the blue, but despite my distrust of other people, I really had no choice but to answer honestly. I told him I did but did not have a job, so I could not pay any rent now. He said he had a room we could stay in, and I could pay him when I found a job. I didn't want to trust him, but I had to. I took a chance, this time with my eyes wide open, and I was going to make this work and hope for the best.

He asked me a lot of questions during the drive. I was terrified that I had gotten into the car with a stranger, with my children. I told him a bit about myself and explained why I was there alone with my two children. He told me that he had a big family with a wife and kids. I was relieved that he was a family man; it made me feel as if I had made the right choice and that my kids would be safe.

There was a large closet in the master bedroom that he had set up as a room for us, and they said we could stay there until I got on my feet. I didn't know what to expect, so I just observed my surroundings and stayed cautious. It was kind of an awkward living situation, but I was so thankful they had opened their home to us.

His wife cooked amazing meals, we were warm, and they were always so kind. During one of those meals, he told me there was a job opening at his friend's bar that I should go apply for. I went and was hired that day and found a nice lady who lived down the street to babysit the kids when I went to work. I was so thankful to have her watching Jake and Emilce because she was very safe, and the kids had food and a roof over their heads while I was working. On my first day, I made $245 in tips!

I worked there for about a year and made enough to get on my feet and find a room for rent. I had enough to pay the babysitter and take my kids out on the weekends. I soon became a supervisor and worked fifteen hours a day, from opening to closing time. After a while, I started to dislike the bar scene and hardly had time with my kids, and I missed being with them. My boss also had me work at the dance club on the weekends to bartend.

It was scary when people got into fights. Once, there was a huge fight between groups, with bottles flying everywhere as I hid under the counter. I thought of my kids and how I did not see them enough. I felt this job was not worth getting hurt over. I came home after a long night and looked at my kids with so much love and felt so much worry I knew I had to do something.

I was also fed up with watching men getting wasted and blowing all their money at the bar while their wives were home with the kids. I knew their wives had to be upset that they were spending their paychecks on alcohol and spending long nights there instead of at home with the family. One day, I was called into the office at the bar, and I was sort of nervous as to why. My boss began talking about how I was a single mother and it must be hard. I thought to myself, *This is the moment I've been waiting for! All my hard work will pay off!* He said there was a way for me to earn extra money, and I thought, *Wait, earn? I'm not getting a raise?*

He said I could do some sexual things with him to earn extra cash, and I was so angry and told him I didn't do those types of things and never would! I was so offended and hurt by what he suggested that I left the office in a hurry. I had too much respect for myself to ever do those types of things for money. That night at the bar, I thought to myself that I didn't deserve this type of treatment and I never saw my kids for this job. Why was I there?

I knew I could do better somewhere else. I looked in the cash register and took all the money that was in there. I went to the office and took the money that was left in there too. I knew it was not right, but in my mind, I thought he owed me for treating me that way, so I took what I deserved. I was leaving this job, so I had to make sure I had enough money to make it to the next job.

At that time, I found another place to rent because the other family I was renting from moved to another place. I looked for another job and ended up working at a deli. Money was not so good, but it got me through until I could find a different job that paid more.

One day, I was invited to a party with a friend, and we had to sleep over because they were drinking, and there was no one sober but me. I had no car and was unable to drive home, and I was too scared to anyway. My friend told me that the kids and I were able to sleep in our own room. I felt better in the way that we could stay away from others while they were drinking. The kids fell asleep, and as I was dozing off, a man came into the room and whispered, "It is going to be okay. It's okay." I got up fast and looked at the kids, and he told me again it would be okay.

I was not sure what he meant by that until he started to take his pants off. I became numb all over and looked at the kids and thought if I fought back, it would wake up the kids and scare them. I froze as he raped me, keeping my eyes closed to go to another place. I could not feel a thing, and when he was done, he whispered in my ear, "I always respected you." He said it in a sick way as if, since he was nice about raping me, it was okay. He got dressed and whispered it again and walked out of the room.

As I lay there, I thought to myself, *At least it was quick, and it was not violent,* never thinking of going to the police. I knew then that I would never put my kids in that position again, so I did not go to parties or sleepovers because I was afraid of having that happen again.

In that time frame, I landed in another bad situation, forgetting what had happened to me a few months earlier. I was at the house where I rented the room, and it was New Year's Eve. They were giving out shots of tequila. I was not a drinker, but I thought, *What the hell, it's one shot.* The man said to take one more. I did not want to, but he convinced me to.

I took it and later woke up naked on the sofa. I got up and fell, as I was so hung over. I hurt all over, and my head had lumps. I was so afraid of where the kids were, so I crawled my way to the room and saw them sleeping. I was confused as to what happened. I started feeling better and walked to the kitchen to see if I could remember.

One of the women who lived there at the house said I was with the guys that night and in a room with them. I asked what had happened, and she told me, "You were having fun."

"I never do those types of things," I told her. I was so confused because I only took two shots of tequila. I felt I was drugged because

I didn't remember anything. I was hurting all over and noticed I was bruised, and my head had a lump. Putting two and two together, I knew I had been raped. I went to the restroom and saw one of the men who was there that night. He looked at me with a smile and said, "You were fun last night." I was so scared and confused.

I was told by the owner of the house that I had to leave immediately. I told her I'd just paid the rent, and she said she wanted me to move out, and I was not getting my rent money back. I went to my room and noticed I had been robbed. The money I had been saving for my own apartment was gone. I asked where it was, and she told me to just leave the house.

I was so angry and left feeling cursed. I did not understand why I was not able to be truly happy and successful. All I wanted was for my kids to have a stable environment and for me to stop being hurt by others. No matter what I did, I ended up nowhere. I stayed at a hotel and paid for a week's stay. As I entered our room, I looked at the nasty curtains and blankets that smelled like cigarettes. I had this feeling of helplessness and dropped to my knees. I cried like I never had before. I had a nervous breakdown.

I asked the man in charge of this cold world to at least help my kids, and I was trying so hard to give them a life. I yelled out, "I hate you for what you are putting us through!" I had never felt like I did that day; the pain was unbearable. I'd always had hope and felt I was always going to make it out. I just could not take it anymore. I looked at my kids and felt this strong urge to keep fighting, and I had to because I wanted them to have a good life.

I had to quit my job because I had this issue of not having a stable place for my kids or enough money to pay a babysitter. I was running out of money to keep paying the hotel for the week, and I kept asking for an extra day to stay until I could gather the money. The man was kind enough to let me stay one more day. I did not have anywhere to go, and I was broke with no money to pay for the hotel or food for the kids. I closed my eyes and took a deep breath and heard someone at the door.

I peeked out the curtain and saw a good friend of mine, the friend who had told me not to go to Costa Rica because I would get hurt. I was shocked with joy! I opened the door, and he looked at me and said, "Wow, you look like shit!" I was so happy he was there at that right time.

    I asked him how he knew I was there, and he said a friend at the bar told him he had seen me and the kids at the hotel, and he felt he had to come and take us to his house. I was so thankful and thanked God for giving me another chance to make a better life for my children. I do not know if "God" was listening to my prayers or if it was my internal faith in myself that I was going to make it out, but whatever it was, I was thankful. This time, I was going to make it happen. Our life was going to get better from that moment on.

Chapter 19

The Job That Changed It All

I MADE IT MY MISSION TO FIND my own place and get a better job. I spoke with a lady who said she had a job opening at California Autism Foundation (CAF). I did not know what sort of work they did, but I sure was happy. I went to the interview with my kids because I did not have a babysitter or help with watching my kids. I was so nervous, as my kids were running all over the place, and I felt it would cost me the job. I had no choice but to bring them, and I was not going to miss this important opportunity. I was told what my duties would be at CAF as well as the mission statement:

To provide people with autism and other developmental disabilities the best possible opportunities for lifetime support, training, and assistance to help them reach their highest potential for independence, productivity, and fulfillment.

They provide vocational training and a social enrichment program. I learned that 88 percent of people with developmental disabilities in the United States are unemployed. The CAF operates an employment program called Custom Assembly & Packaging (CAP) that provides assembly, labeling, packaging, and fulfillment services to different businesses.

There were things I would have to learn during my probationary period at CAF:

- Working with consumers on daily hygiene (body and clothing);
- Daily charting on each of my consumers;
- Giving instructions;
- Giving directions;
- Settling small disputes;
- Ensuring quality control of 100 percent of the product completed;
- Directing a consumer to the office if the consumer is not responding to my request;
- Writing incident reports when needed;
- Having current CPR and first-aid certificate on file;
- Responding to seizures as quickly as possible, complete with paperwork; and
- Learning to train the consumer on how to do jobs that come in.[1]

The manager told me I was very lucky she had given me an interview at all. I asked her why, and she looked at me like I was crazy and said, "Who would bring their kids to an interview and with their kids running everywhere?" I told her I was thankful and filled her in on my situation. She looked at me and told me she was getting herself into a mess but was going to give me a chance. My heart dropped, and I was so happy!

I was set up to get childcare help for low-income families. Free childcare a block away from the job was too good to be true. La Petite Academy was a school that accepted kids from infants to kindergarten. It was clean and safe. They were fed and able to take naps, plus I got a progress note at the end of every day. Our lives were changing for the better, but I was so afraid because I knew how cursed I was.

---

[1] California Autism Foundation, Accessed October 21, 2022, http://calautism.org/

At work, I was a mess emotionally. I did not trust anyone, and I blocked out those who were trying to get to know me. I cut conversations short and gave no eye contact at all. Soon after, they made fun of me for it and said I was "stuck up." I think it was because I did not gossip or give them the time of day. I was there to work, not to gossip about others at work.

I had another nervous breakdown due to stress while working and wound up in the hospital. I told them how I was feeling, and they asked a bit about my background. I told them what I had gone through as a child and in my past marriage. They said I had complex post-traumatic stress disorder (CPTSD). I did not know what that was or how people ended up with it. All I knew was I was unable to handle stress. I didn't like it to be quiet, and I liked to keep busy. When it was quiet, it gave me room to think, and all I thought about were my mother's, Earl's, and Ramon's voices. I felt the pain of their words like I was reliving the moments over and over and over! I was afraid of not making it this time and losing my job. I wondered if we were going to be on the streets the next day or if someone was going to hurt me again. I was a mess and knew I needed help.

The doctors took a drug test on me and saw that I did not do drugs. They asked if I drank alcohol, and I said no. We talked a lot about CPTSD and what steps to take to manage it. I was prescribed Zoloft for depression and CPTSD. It took a few weeks to feel the effects. I had people telling me that I was not as stuck up as before, and I looked as if I had slept. I felt amazing from not panicking as much, and I was able to wake up in the morning feeling better than ever.

I used to feel like I had been hit by a car when I woke up, and I was often depressed. I went to therapy once a week for a few months until I was good enough to go once a month. I was feeling great and started to give life another chance. I went dancing on Friday nights and had friends I talked to, but from a distance. I was not ready to let people into my life personally, so I never let anyone get too close to me or my kids. I loved doing things for others because it made me feel good, but I did not like others to do any favors for me. I hated to feel I owed someone for helping me. Learning to keep my distance seemed to be working for me, and I kept it that way.

I was learning so much about autism and other types of disabilities. I felt sorry for them when I started working with them, but soon after, I was amazed at how proud I was of them. They kept trying and never worried about what others thought because they knew they had something special that no one else had.

They sometimes took advantage of their disabilities to get away with things that were not so good. I quickly knew everyone's personality. I knew how to work with them on their goals each day. I soon included them all in my life as if they were my kids. I loved working for CAF because it gave me a purpose and more confidence.

My boss, Jeannette, even wrote a letter about my transformation:

> On the day Jessica came to interview at the California Autism Foundation, we met in the student classroom at the rear of the warehouse. She came in the door followed by two small children—I thought, *What is she thinking?* She then explained how she had no one to leave her kids with and did not want to miss the interview, as she really needed a job.
>
> She went on to explain about being a single parent who was living day to day. As we were talking, she introduced the children to me as Jake and Emilce. They were doing their best to sit quietly, but that lasted all of five minutes, and they spent the rest of the interview running from one part of the room to the other, with Jessica asking them to sit down! Even at this early stage, I felt that these two children were very attracted to each other and very hyper-active.
>
> I also strongly felt that Jessica came to me at this time for a reason, and she needed to be helped.

I made up my mind to hire her, and hoped it would work out, knowing we had a lot of work ahead. All the staff and supervisors were a working team; all were expected to work together.

At the time we had approximately fifty consumers, all with developmental or physical disabilities. I cautioned Jessica to be a mentor and teacher, not their mother, we were to make them independent, not dependent on us. She agreed. Her honeymoon period was ninety days. She learned a lot during this time.

One lesson was, just because a person is [slow] does not mean they are without knowledge and that they don't know how to fool you or set you up. In the beginning, the consumers who wanted to get away with anything gravitated to Jessica—after a while they left her alone.

It was part of our system to call out the consumers we needed to do the jobs that had to be completed as soon as possible. After roll-call was completed, those who had good eyesight and good coordination were chosen to do the jobs. There was always a group of consumers who did not fit the criteria. These were the ones that Jessica was left with. She complained to me about this but, while I could see her side, the jobs had to be done.

Our customers would not wait, and quality control had to be one hundred percent. Again Jessica came to my office to ask if she could train these consumers to do work that was expected by our vendors. I said yes, but it would be a job that she needed to do while still completing all her other duties. I would say 60% to 70% of the students she trained succeeded and became fully functioning workers, and they were chosen by other staff to work.

There were many times that Jake and Emilce came to work with Jessica. Our rule was, if you can't find a sitter, bring them to work, we will find a way, but never leave your child in a car in our parking lot. So, she would set them up in her office, which was very small, and report to work within ten to fifteen minutes. I could hear the kids running back and forth, chairs screeching and voices saying, "Jake, stop!" and, "Emilce, give me my paper!" I would go to the staff office and warn them maybe twice before I separated them, one in my office and one in the café area, where they were within eyesight of each other. They seemed to have an unspoken language between them. They would burst out laughing as if they had told each other a joke. I saw ADHD in both Jake and Emilce, it seemed to get slightly better as they got older.

Jessica continued to grow. She had some issues with other staff. I felt that her expansion of herself was high, as far as lifestyle went: how to treat others, and how you respond to consumers. So she expected the same from everyone else, and she was disappointed. She complained about this, and I tried to explain that all staff had different aspects of their personalities that were needed. Jessica continued to get more independent in her work and her choices. She became more creative, and made a life-size turkey out of papier-mâché, the consumers loved it. She also made a tree. Every Thanksgiving, her turkey was front and center on the display, and after she left the program, we continued to use that turkey.

Jessica came in to ask for a meeting, so I scheduled one for the next day. She came in, very confident, stated all the accomplishments she had achieved in the past year, and asked for a raise. We were a non-profit, and money was always an issue, but she was given a small raise after her review. (By the way, Jessica, I am shocked that you still have that written review! That proves that the word is a very powerful thing, when used in either a good or a bad way!)

We celebrated all holidays at CAF with the consumers and their families. Jessica was always willing to take an active part in decorating and helping set up and clean up. One thing was very clear throughout all the years Jessica was employed with us. She was a mother first, and always thought of her kids in everything she did, and through the years Jake and Emilce remained very close, with a bond that I felt would never be broken, not even now with her gone.

So, Jessica, from the wide-eyed naive person I first met, to the woman I spoke to last week, you have come a long way, and with the hand you were dealt, you need to pat yourself on the back, as you have accomplished much, and with the road now laced with grief, you will be challenged. So remember, grief shared is grief diminished, speak of Emilce often, as if she were still here. She mattered. She was loved, and she knew this... I am proud of you and Jake.

Love always,

Jeanette

CHAPTER 20

A Wonderful Man

I MET A WONDERFUL MAN NAMED GUILLERMO while I was working at CAF. He worked in the shipping department. He always went out of his way to say hi to me, so I tried to avoid him as much as possible, feeling as if he was trying too hard, and that intimidated me. I was ready to date at the time but had never thought of him as a possibility.

We passed by each other at work until one day, he told me, "Happy birthday!" I laughed, and he asked me where his gift was. I was confused because I didn't understand his weird jokes. He took my hand in his, and butterflies fluttered within my stomach, and I felt like it was meant to be. I felt as if he would protect me, and there was a sense of security about him. I let go of all my worries and accepted the fact that it was okay to try again. I really liked this man.

I heard lots of comments from my friends—that I was getting into another relationship too soon, that I was barely getting on my feet, etc. I fought hard with my own mixed emotions about the situation, but when it came down to it, I wanted to feel love! I wanted to have a real friendship and partnership with someone who loved me!

My children were my main concern. What was going to be best for them? After a few months of dating Guillermo, I noticed that he had a very special bond with my Emilce, who was two at the time. They played together, and she brushed his hair. He was perfect with her.

Jake was five years old at the time, and with him, it was a little bit of a different story. He was very protective of me, and when Guillermo was around, Jake wanted all my attention. When Guillermo noticed this, he did his best to be accepted by my son and bought him a scooter. The gift took me by surprise. I was shocked that he would go out of his way like that for a five-year-old who was not his own. Jake started to really like him, watch cartoons with him, and play with him.

The day came when we finally moved in together, and it was also the day I realized how traumatized I still was by my past. I started having bad dreams and anxiety about the house being perfect all the time. I panicked that the food wasn't good enough or my kids weren't behaving well enough. I even worried that I wasn't good enough in bed!

I felt so alone in what I wanted, whatever that even was. I felt useless, like there was this weight inside me preventing me from being truly happy. I asked Guillermo if he ever felt the way I did, and I saw he was confused. He was kind of avoiding my personal emotions because he didn't really understand.

I had a job and busted my butt for my kids, and I had a nice man in my life who cared about them too, but inside, I was in agony. I had so much insecurity, and I hated my past. I thought people would judge me for it if they knew about it and how I grew up. I felt like I did not deserve happiness and was never going to feel real happiness. I wanted help so badly because the pain I had suppressed for so many years had become unbearable. The feeling of being alone because no one understood the flashbacks I had, or the feeling of wanting to be normal like everyone else, made it even worse.

I started going to a psychologist and told him everything, explaining all the details of my life that I had never really spoken out loud before. I thought I was so messed up that I could never be fixed and that I didn't deserve to be in a relationship. I wanted my pain to end so I could be a stronger person and trust someone with all my heart. I didn't want to push this amazing man I now had out of my life because of my issues.

I thought of my children and how I didn't want to break the happiness that completed them by having a stable father figure in their lives. I wasn't sure what I needed, and I was willing to do everything to get better, even if that meant I had to see a therapist every day.

Chapter 21

Working on Me

I CONTINUED WITH THERAPY, AND THEY ASKED me why I stayed with Guillermo if I didn't trust him. The only answer I had was that I had to give it another try for my kids and me to live a happy life. I had to trust myself to trust it would work if I got the help I needed. I could not handle my emotions with all my thoughts and fears. I was always ready to find something wrong so I could have a reason to leave and be alone with my kids, to avoid feeling afraid of what the other person would do next to hurt me.

This was the hardest time in my life, full of depression and anxiety. There were a lot of ups and downs. I was very angry because I thought no one understood me, and no one understood what it was like not to have a family to turn to. I felt like a bad mother every holiday and birthday since my kids had no family to enjoy it with them. I did not enjoy many things, as everything reminded me of all the bad that had happened during my childhood. I wound up getting angry with myself for getting angry with Guillermo because he did not understand me or how I felt. I started to think I was an unfit mother who should not have kids since I did not have a good upbringing.

Guillermo did not have any children of his own, and he took on the responsibility of being an amazing father figure to my two wonderful children. He was so amazing with them, and I was so happy to have him around.

At one of my appointments, while talking to my therapist, I was asked if I had ever gone to visit any of my other family members. I had not because I felt I did not fit in or was not wanted due to my mother being the victim and never telling the truth about what it was like growing up in our home. She always made it look like we were bad kids.

My therapist reminded me that I was an adult, able to go see my family and let them decide how they felt about me, and suggested I visit my grandpa, whom I loved very much. I put a lot of thought into it and decided to go look for him. Guillermo helped me so much and went with me. Jake and Emilce were so excited to see him, too, and I hoped that we were not thrown off his property because he did not want me around. The whole ride there, I struggled with how I was feeling and thinking. What if he told me I was a bad child and wanted me to leave? What if I was not good enough to be part of the family? What if my mom ruined every possible way of even being able to explain myself because he would believe her over me? What if and what if?

We pulled up to his driveway and parked. Guillermo said, "We are here," with a smile. I took a deep breath as I walked up to his door. I knocked, with so many thoughts and feelings flowing through my body. As he opened his door, my stomach gurgled in anticipation of seeing his face and hearing his voice.

I took a deep breath and said, "Hi, Grandpa. It's me, Jessica."

My grandpa said, "Jessica?"

He looked so amazing for his age, and I wanted to just hug him at that moment. I held myself back and told him I wanted to see him and show him my family. He asked me lots of questions and ended up really loving Guillermo.

They talked about war and politics. I was so happy that they got along, and soon it felt like a normal relationship. I went every weekend or so to eat lunch and talk. I never talked about my mother and my past until I felt I needed to. Then he told me I was upsetting him, and he did not want to see his daughter in that way. I respected his wish and went on to talk about amazing things that were positive. My aunt was very suspicious of why I was there, and I told her I was just there to visit him. She ended up accepting me and my family.

One day, I got a phone call from my mother. I wondered how she got my number and asked her, and she said my grandpa had given it to her. She called to let me know that Earl had cancer, and she wanted me to pray for him. I asked why she wanted me, of all people, to do that. She said for what they had done to me, it was important that I forgive them in case they should die. She said she would go to hell if I didn't. I felt so sick emotionally that I had to hang up on her. Then I felt so guilty for doing that and decided to call her back. I told her I felt bad for him, with a feeling of disgust, and forgave them for what they did. I lied through my teeth just to please them. I did this all the time, telling people what they wanted to hear just so they would be happy and leave me alone. I put myself down so they'd feel better.

I went to talk with my therapist and told her about my mom calling me and what she wanted from me. My therapist said something I would never forget: "You have a right to be angry and don't have to pretend you are not just to make them feel better. You have the right to say, 'I don't want to talk to you anymore,' even if they are your family. You can forgive, but you will never forget, and this is why it is important to stop talking to those who cause you to have triggers." I remember feeling very weak and drained emotionally whenever my mom called just to pretend we were all good with what had happened and could somehow work on a relationship we never had.

She called, and I was ready to tell my mom how I felt. I said I forgave her but was unable to continue talking to her. She was so upset and asked why. I told her I felt sick when we talked and it gave me triggers. I said it took me a week to feel better after contact with her. She said she should kill herself, and I realized this was all to make me feel guilty. I told her I was sorry and hung up. She called so many times and left so many messages, so I changed my number. Since then, I told my grandpa not to give my number out, and that was the last I heard from my mom. I learned how to say no and mean what

I say without feeling guilty. I felt a huge wave of relief and started to notice a difference in me emotionally.

I still felt I did not fit in with the normal world, like an outsider. I could not handle stress or excitement without going numb and dissociating. I hated how I was feeling when out in public because I believed they could see how I was feeling, and I wanted to run away. I often forgot where I was and who I was, and it lasted around five minutes or so but felt like an eternity. I often fell into a state of panic at stores, and it happened only when I was alone. It was so scary. I knew what was wrong with me and that I was not going crazy: it was me having complex PTSD, and it was going to be this way when I got excited or scared. I just had to learn to let go and know these feelings would pass. I started to think of positive things and pushed myself out of that state of mind.

After a year, I applied for a divorce from Ramon, filing everything on my own. I felt so good that day when I went to family court because I was stronger, another step toward being truly free. The court system took a few months, but when the divorce was final and I no longer had his last name, I was Jessica Williams again—and oh, man, did that sound good! I got full custody of the kids, and I thought I could take on the world. Sometimes when filling out forms where I had to sign my name, I forgot I had changed it to Jessica Williams and used my old name. It took practice to remember that I no longer had that old last name.

After a few months, Guillermo asked me to marry him, but having just gotten out of a marriage, I kind of liked my new freedom and my own last name. It was hard to think about going through another marriage and trusting again. It was a difficult choice at the time. I finally said yes, and we got married on February 14, 2006, when I was six months pregnant with my daughter Isabelle. We eventually had two beautiful daughters together: Isabelle, born on June 18, 2006, Father's Day; and Evelynn, born on December 25, 2010, Christmas morning. They were the best gifts. We ended up with four kids, and Guillermo loved all the kids equally. I couldn't have been luckier. Sure, we had disagreements, like most marriages, but at the end of the day, he was so supportive and loving. My kids loved him as a father, and he loved the kids as much as they loved him.

Jake was very talkative, with lots of energy, so he made friends everywhere he went. Jake had that special personality that everyone seemed to love being around. Emilce had a mind of an entrepreneur; she wanted to study fashion and learn how to make her own cosmetic brand. Emilce was also an amazing photographer and always saw the beauty in everything. Isabelle was highly creative, loved to read, and had amazing goals in her life—beyond her years. Evelynn was very open and talkative; she knew what she wanted and did things her way. The kids never followed others, and they knew who they were as people, and I loved who they were. I was very lucky to have amazing kids and a great man in my life. I had always wanted a family of my own, to become a mother who would do anything for her kids. They made my life complete.

Years went by, and we worked hard to get our lives together and kept succeeding. We had moved a few times but eventually settled down in our own house. The kids were growing and doing what kids do best. I loved being their mother and being there for them.

I started to get into gardening. I had lots of fruit trees, vegetables, shrubs, and flowers. I really loved spending time in the garden because it helped with depression. Guillermo and I did many projects together and spent a lot of quality time in the yard, worked on cars, and cooked together. I noticed I stayed in reality more and had something positive to focus on. I also had lots of animals, mostly rescues: a Vietnamese potbellied pig, a rooster, hens, tortoises, a bearded dragon, a cat, fish, and two dogs. I loved animals, and giving them a good home made me happy.

Chapter 22

Grieving

LIFE TOOK A TURN FOR THE WORST when Emilce ended up with leukemia at the age of fifteen. She was diagnosed in April 2014 and passed away a few months later, in June 2014. Life was not supposed to happen like this. I fought so hard to give her the life she deserved. I wanted Emilce to live her dreams.

She wanted to start her own brand and said she was going to give back in a big way. Even when she was sick, she thought of others and said if she survived, she was going to live life to the fullest and help others. She really was the sweetest and most positive girl anyone could have ever met.

After Emilce's passing, things got hard for the family. I had to stay strong to be there for everyone. I cried when they were asleep at night and went through the worst heartache I had ever experienced. I became very depressed but did not want to show it on the outside, so I kept all the pain inside. Over the years, I never really coped with her passing, and I became this person I did not recognize. I used to have so much hope and optimism. I just felt more angry than sad. The anger I had was so excruciating. I stopped talking to people and stopped doing interviews on the story of my past, and I used to have so much passion for helping others. I stopped feeling like I wanted to help others because I could not help myself from feeling the way I did.

I gave up on every dream and goal I had, and it was not a good feeling. I felt so empty because I believed I had failed as a mother. I wished I could have done something to save her from her cancer, and I questioned whether I was the cause of her leukemia. The guilt was so powerful that it took over my life. I was so angry and hated myself for so long after she passed. I could not sleep at night, most of the time lying on the sofa or the floor. I had so much pain inside, so many nightmares of when we had to pull the plug, seeing her lifeless body and the way it felt when she passed. I remember whispering in her ear that I was so proud of her and she could go rest now. I remember how sweet she smelled and how innocent she looked. She didn't deserve this, and I felt so angry. I never thought one of my kids would die before me, never thought I was going to be that mother whose child died of cancer.

I changed inside, but it did not stop me from being a mother and a wife. I put my family first before dealing with what I was feeling. At night, I cried and broke down in another room so they wouldn't see. I wanted to be alone and not be around anyone at night because that was the time when it was quiet, and I could not stand that it was quiet because it gave me room to think. I had anxiety and panic attacks from all the memories.

Even though I talked to Guillermo about what I was feeling, he never understood what pain I was in. I could not give him the amount of attention he needed 100 percent of the time. Soon after, Guillermo told me he did not want to be in this marriage and he'd had an affair. He said we didn't work together and he was not getting the attention he once had.

I knew I had changed since Emilce's passing, and I had always worked on my past traumas to avoid letting them affect my marriage and how I raised my kids. I thought that was enough to keep my marriage strong. I believed that not getting the help I needed to grieve Emilce's passing affected my marriage. We had been married for seventeen years, and we had our ups and downs, but never like this.

I went through the worst emotional pain since Emilce's passing. I was now grieving the death of my marriage. The anger I had toward him was so unbearable. The pain from being so angry killed me inside. I thought it was so selfish of him to leave me at the worst time of my life. He knew what I was going through because I would tell him often. He was my best friend that knew everything about me. I was so disappointed and disgusted that he'd been with another while I was in pain. I guess he had needs that I could not meet.

I dropped the kids off at school and tried hard not to show how much emotional pain I was in. As they walked off to class, I thought of how much I loved them and felt that I'd failed them as a mother because I could not keep their father happy and I could not keep Emilce alive. *I failed them*, I kept thinking to myself.

I got home, where I broke down and cried like I never had before. I sat there on the kitchen floor, thinking it would be better if I just died, and then maybe the pain would go away. I thought to myself, *How much can a person take until they break for good?* I had never in my life broken down so hard this way. I talked to God and asked him to shield me from this agony I was feeling.

I thought I was a failure as a child, a failure as a mother, and now a failure as a wife. I felt I'd failed everything in life. I was so afraid of doing what I thought was best at the time. I did not want my kids to see me like this, and I had to be strong for them. For four months straight, I had episodes where I would be crying, and I had this uncontrollable laugh. I could not stop laughing and crying at the same time. I remember when I had these episodes, I would hide in my closet so the kids would not see me. I was broken inside, and I was so scared I was not going to come out of this mental breakdown. All I knew was I did not want to feel this pain and anger any longer. I started to work on my mental health and did a lot of inner healing on my own until I could not do it alone. After a year, I stopped avoiding what I was feeling and made my appointment to see a psychiatrist. I told her everything that had happened.

She said I had PTSD but also bipolar depression. I did not want to hear I was bipolar. The psychiatrist explained my repeated record of ups and downs through the years to me. She said it seemed I had bipolar depression. I saw the chart with a pattern over the years, and I was at my last straw in life and did not want to feel like I was feeling anymore. All I wanted was for them to heal me from the emotional pain I was in.

I really wanted to put my trust in the psychiatrist, but I was scared. I did not want this diagnosis at the worst time in my life. It just added more agony in a way because having something like bipolar depression made me feel ashamed and weak. It made me feel like I was unable to handle myself like a normal person. I told her I had kids and could not be bipolar and medicated. I needed to be there for them! I knew I had taken Zoloft, which helped with PTSD, depression and anxiety, but that was not as embarrassing as taking bipolar medication.

She explained so much to me about bipolar disorder. She said some of the most successful, creative people had bipolar disorder, and there was nothing wrong with that. She was so helpful. I was no longer ashamed. I did my research and educated myself. I was so wrong for feeling embarrassed or ashamed about having bipolar depression.

I decided to take the medication that was prescribed: Latuda. I was afraid of taking such a drug due to possible side effects, like addiction or weight gain. I imagined it making me super sleepy, mentally unbalanced, or unable to take care of my kids. I had to be there 100 percent of the time.

I started feeling huge relief within a few weeks. I had never felt so good. I was no longer seemingly dying inside. So happy, I called my psychiatrist and thanked her for everything, especially for helping me with my depression. Life was good again, and I felt the warm sun hitting my skin for the first time in so long.

Many months went by, and I had not had an episode of depression, though sometimes I feared its return. There are no words to describe how thankful I was to the therapist, the psychiatrist, and all mental-health doctors. If you let them help you and you do the work to get your mental health on track, you can live an amazing life. My life has changed since starting my treatment.

I spent a few years of therapy, learning how to live life after infidelity. I learned how to deal with grief, and I still see a therapist to deal with my childhood trauma. It is a lot of work, but it is worth every minute. I've learned so much, and I am truly thankful for the support I've received. It took so much work to get to a positive place in my life after all I'd been through.

Not a day goes by that I do not think of Emilce. I miss her with all my heart, and I know she is watching from above. I will continue to live my life to the fullest for Emilce. Everywhere I look, I see her. She is the beauty of blooming flowers. She is the breeze against the trees, the flowing water in rivers. She is the air I breathe. She saw so much beauty when she was here and always captured it. Her photography was amazing. I will always try to see the world as she saw it. She inspired me so much. I will always think of her, and I will always love her.

I have worked on my marriage to keep all of us together. It was not easy! Marriage takes hard work to keep it alive. We will always love each other, and we love our kids deeply. We are a family and will be there for one another for life. People change, and that's okay. I learned that I can't change what happens in life, but I can always change the way I respond to it.

I often think of my childhood, and I am proud of the little girl who endured so much in her life. I am proud of the little girl who kept getting up when they kicked her down. I am so proud of that little girl who did not let them destroy her. I am so grateful that my inner child broke free! I am free from abuse and toxic people. I am free to live a life of good and positivity.

I have taken the high road and let go of so many things from my past. I focus on what matters most in life. I won't let what others do affect my life and my well-being. I am living my life with a full heart because I know how fragile life is and that it can be over in the blink of an eye. I know I deserve to be happy, and I will make the most of every blessing I receive. After everything I have been through in this life, I am truly thankful that I survived and continue to thrive.

Chapter 23

What I Have Learned through It All

TELLING MY STORY CHANGED MY LIFE. IF I had not spoken out and hadn't told what happened to me, I would have stayed in the same depressive state. I would still be asking myself, "Why me?" I would have never understood that other people have endured similar trauma or much worse. I did not talk to or trust many people. I avoided everything that made me uncomfortable. I could not escape the memories of my past and pretended they did not affect me. I was in agony and hated everything about me. The feeling of not being whole, not knowing who you are in life, and not knowing the purpose of all the pain just makes wanting to keep living harder. I'd had enough of that kind of mindset. I was not going to live my life in agony any longer. I took the steps to climb out of the funk I was in and get the help I needed.

What I learned from my experiences was that I had to be resilient. I had to look at the positives and keep pushing for greatness. When bad things happen in my life, I never let them change who I really am inside. I learned to stay away from toxic people and how to say no and mean it. I learned that everything I'd been through was not my fault. I learned how to love myself and put myself first.

Finding a way to make peace with your past and deal with your anger, sadness, worry, regret, confusion, hopelessness, or whatever it may be through writing, music, art, dance, mentoring, speaking, and so many other amazing ways can help you get out of that negative mindset. Others will then find their way through you. However you express what you went through is your journey and yours alone. No one can take that creativity from you. Your story is very special, with a purpose.

I want people to move forward to become who they truly are by inspiring them to find the help they need or gain the courage to leave their bad situations. I love watching people grow into beautiful individuals who will touch others with their stories, courage, and strength. I want to hear their stories about how this book helped them. I want people to make changes to break free. I want to see everyone grow from their experiences and live! I made it out alive, and I am still standing—for that, I am truly grateful.

About the Author

Jessica Solsona, author of *Diabolical in Disguise*, is from the Bay Area, California. She has four wonderful kids and an amazing husband. She loves to garden, and she has many fruit trees. She has lots of animals that keep her busy as much as the kids do. She states with joy, "I am so thankful I am free from abuse and live the life I always wanted. I wrote this memoir in hopes it will help someone."

Printed in the USA
CPSIA information can be obtained
at www.ICGtesting.com
LVHW050437190823
755495LV00002B/309